Michael Ots is one of the most gift
trustworthiness and authenticity o
the universities of Europe. In this k
to honest questions raised by those
message of Jesus Christ is true and
looking for evidences, it is a great p
answers may change your life!
Lindsay Brown, International Director, Lausanne Movement for World Evangelisation

This latest from Michael's pen has all the hallmarks of a great introduction to the Christian faith. It's widely researched, easy to read, brilliantly illustrated and (to quote Francis Schaeffer) it gives 'honest answers to honest questions'. *But Is It True?* takes the reader on a fascinating journey of enquiry, dealing with issues of doubt, science, psychology and ancient history, before arriving at the heart of the Christian faith, a detailed study of Jesus himself. You can tell that Michael is an experienced university speaker, as he never runs too far ahead of us, hoping we'll all catch up. Rather, with patience and humility, he prefers to get alongside us, engagingly guiding the reader's quest with equal expertise and enthusiasm. I look forward to using this book at our church!
Dave Gobbett, Lead Minister, Highfields Church, Cardiff, and Word Alive trustee

In this original and thought-provoking book Michael Ots shows how the biases that distort human reasoning affect all of us – atheists, sceptics and believers alike. We need to acknowledge, but not be overwhelmed by, these realities, and Ots argues compellingly that reason, intellect and reflection are still the friends, and not the enemies, of authentic faith.
Glynn Harrison, Emeritus Professor of Psychiatry, University of Bristol

In this book Michael Ots presents a powerful cumulative case for the truth of Christianity. In a light and easy-to-read style he exposes the many weaknesses of New Atheist arguments and skilfully demonstrates the vastly superior explanatory power of Christian theism. I heartily recommend this book for believer and atheist alike.
The Revd Dr Rodney D. Holder, The Faraday Institute, St Edmund's College, Cambridge

But Is It True? is unusually well written, weaving stories with logical discourse and evidence. Finding its roots in today's questions, the book branches into modern cinema, philosophy, science and art, setting forth easily understood answers to the questions many are raising. Beginning with the tenet that 'No-one wants to believe a delusion, no matter how good it makes you feel', Michael Ots gives you good reasons for believing, challenging those who believe that atheism explains reality.

Mark Lanier, one of America's top trial lawyers, author of Christianity on Trial *and founder of the Lanier Theological Library*

Did Jesus really live? Are the stories the Gospels tell about him true? Did he really rise from the grave? Is there any valid reason to doubt that these are historical facts? Michael Ots leads the way through the maze of reasons for doubt or disbelief, arguing that believing brings understanding of the extraordinary teacher and his significance today.

Alan Millard, Emeritus Rankin Professor of Hebrew and Ancient Semitic Languages, University of Liverpool

Objections to the Christian faith come thick and fast, but Michael Ots demonstrates how weak they often turn out to be. Tackling a number of common questions, Michael blends rigorous research with an accessible style in order to present formidable and winsome answers. Do you question the Christian faith? Let this book guide your search for answers!

Chris Sinkinson, Lecturer in Old Testament and Apologetics, Moorlands College, Christchurch, UK

BUT IS IT TRUE?

MICHAEL OTS

BUT IS IT TRUE?

Honest responses to 10 popular objections to the Christian faith

ivp

INTER-VARSITY PRESS
36 Causton Street, London SW1P 4ST, England
Email: ivp@ivpbooks.com
Website: www.ivpbooks.com

British Library Cataloguing in Publication Data
A catalogue record for this book is available from the British Library.

ISBN: 978–1–78359–404–7

Set in Dante 12/15pt
Typeset in Great Britain by CRB Associates, Potterhanworth, Lincolnshire

Inter-Varsity Press publishes Christian books that are true to the Bible and that communicate the gospel, develop discipleship and strengthen the church for its mission in the world.

IVP originated within the Inter-Varsity Fellowship, now the Universities and Colleges Christian Fellowship, a student movement connecting Christian Unions in universities and colleges throughout Great Britain, and a member movement of the International Fellowship of Evangelical Students. Website: www.uccf.org.uk. That historic association is maintained, and all senior IVP staff and committee members subscribe to the UCCF Basis of Faith.

CONTENTS

ACKNOWLEDGMENTS

This book started life as a series of talks that I have given in different universities across Europe. I am thankful to the many atheists and sceptics whose questions, comments and feedback have stretched me to think more deeply on all these issues, as well as to the Christian students who were bold enough to organize such public events.

One of the great things about writing a book is that there are no rules about where you have to do the work! So, as well as sitting in my office at home, parts of this book were also written in a beach hut in Bournemouth, a summerhouse in Cornwall and a campsite by a lake in New Zealand. Thank you so much to those whose generosity and hospitality made this possible.

Writing this book has definitely been a team effort, and I am deeply grateful to those who have taken so much time in reading the manuscripts and whose input has vastly improved the material. Thanks to Peter Dray, Jürgen Spieß, Lindsay Brown, Michael Green, Simon Wenham, Chris Sinkinson, Rodney Holder, Alan Millard, Lizzie Coyle, Christine Dillon,

Alex Holt, Ricardo Costa and Tim Dixon. A special thanks to Tom Welton, Josh Fountain, Chris Oldfield and Gareth Leaney, who have participated in numerous phone calls, emails and meetings to discuss various parts!
I think my old English teachers would have been highly amused to know that I have gone on to write a book, given my atrocious record at spelling and grammar. I have great respect for those who are multilingual when I don't even know one language very well! I am therefore thankful to those who helped to get this to a place where you might be willing to read it – especially to my very patient editor Eleanor Trotter and my diligent copyeditor Kath Stanton.

Most of all, I am thankful that I know the One about whom I speak and write. It is wonderful to know that God not only exists, but that he also knows me personally and cares for me deeply.

INTRODUCTION

'Does God exist?' had been the title of our debate. The hot and stuffy lecture room was crammed full of inquisitive students who had been quizzing us on what we had already explained in our opening remarks. The discussion had been fun and lively, and, to make matters even more interesting, the whole debate had been simultaneously translated, as my opponent and I were, quite literally, talking different languages!

Our time was nearly up, and all that was left was for each of us to sum up our arguments. Only three minutes were allotted to us, but I was conscious that it was this more than anything else that people would probably remember. I concluded things as well as I felt I could and sat down. It was now my opponent's turn. Three minutes isn't long – especially when you are being translated – but he didn't need them all anyway. He simply said,

It's not that I don't like the idea of Christianity – I'm sure that it gives you great comfort to believe in God and know that he loves you. But my problem is this – *it's not true*! I don't want to believe what is *nice*. I want to believe what is *true*. I'm passionate about the truth!

In one sense I agreed with him . . . though sadly I didn't have the opportunity to say so publicly. If Christianity is not true, then it's not worth believing. No-one wants to believe a delusion, no matter how good it makes you feel.

Ever since I was a teenager, I have tried to engage with the questions of sceptics. If Christianity really is true, then it should stand up to honest questioning. I reasoned that I would either discover that Christianity wasn't true – in which case I would be saved from believing a lie – or I might discover more reasons as to why it was true – and then my faith would grow.

Since then I have discovered that every question and objection to Christianity can really be boiled down to two – 'Is it good?' and 'Is it true?' As I have listened to these questions and sought to find answers to them, I have become increasingly convinced that Christianity is both good *and* true – existentially satisfying *and* intellectually robust. This conviction hasn't come by ignoring those with different opinions from my own, but by engaging with them, something I continue to do on a daily basis in universities across Europe.

In my first book *What Kind of God?* (subsequently translated into Korean, Romanian, Serbian, Russian and Spanish) I attempted to answer the first type of question: 'Is it good?' This will be my attempt to answer the second: *But Is It True?*

However, I am aware that you may be coming to this from a very different starting point. If so, then thank you for being willing to give this book a read! I hope that, at the very least, it encourages you to think through your own objections to Christianity.

My aim has been to keep this book simple without it becoming simplistic. No prior knowledge of any of the subjects should be required. If some of the chapter questions are not an issue for you at the moment, then feel free to start with one that is. Of course, answering one question often raises others in your mind that you hadn't even thought of before. You may then find that these are addressed in other chapters. Inevitably, there is far more to say than could be said in each chapter and covered in a book of this size. For the intrigued, as well as the unconvinced, I have included recommendations for further reading at the end of each chapter.

Obstacles to truth

Before we dive into the first chapter, it may be helpful to give a word of advice. Discovering the truth may not be as easy as we first thought. Let's look at some of the obstacles that we might face in trying to discover truth. For a start, is discovering truth even possible?

Scepticism about truth

Is there such a thing as objective truth at all? On several occasions, after I have given a talk, people have said to me, 'Well, that's true *for you*', the implication being that it didn't also have to be true *for them*. Whereas previous generations spoke about truth in absolute and universal terms, such confidence can seem rather arrogant today. We become suspicious of such claims, and suspect that they are being used to gain power over others.

Yet, while it is right to admit that none of us knows absolutely, that does not mean that there is no such thing as absolute truth. Similarly, it is precisely because truth is important and precious that we are grieved at the way people might abuse it for their own ends. While we should be rightly suspicious of some people's truth claims, and humble about our own limitations, we don't need to doubt the very concept of truth itself.

Imbalance

There are two equal and opposite dangers that we can fall into when it comes to belief. On one side is extreme gullibility – where we end up believing anything. On the other side is extreme scepticism – where we could end up believing nothing. Often, in an attempt to avoid the former, we can end up veering off into the latter. There is nothing wrong with healthy scepticism (that can stop us from believing things that aren't true), but extreme scepticism may stop us from believing the things that are true! We need balance, so that we don't end up believing too much or too little.

Apatheism

In an article in *The Atlantic*, Jonathan Rauch coined the term 'apatheism' to describe our attitude to religious truth. Seeing the dangers of religious extremism, he suggested as the solution a benign indifference to all beliefs. Extreme beliefs are seen as dangerous, and the answer is to be moderate in everything.

The problem with this is that it treats all religious beliefs as the same and neglects to examine the content of any of them. Of course, if a belief were inherently violent, then strong belief would be dangerous and a moderate belief would be preferred, though surely not believing it at all would be even better! But what if your belief was that you should love your enemies and do good to those who persecute you? Surely then it would be better to follow that belief strongly?

The fundamental issue with apatheism is that it breeds laziness with regard to the truth. Novelist Dorothy L. Sayers describes this as 'the sin which believes nothing, cares for nothing, seeks to know nothing, interferes with nothing, enjoys nothing, loves nothing, hates nothing, finds purpose in nothing, lives for nothing, and only remains alive because there is nothing it would die for'.[1]

False tolerance

Closely related to apatheism is another danger – a wrong definition of the word 'tolerance'. Much is made of tolerance in Western society. While tolerance of other ideas is a good thing,[2] its meaning has become confused with the idea that we can never say that anything is wrong. Yet, if I tolerate someone, then it presupposes that we disagree on something. If we did not, then there would be no need for tolerance! While it is understandably popular to suggest that all beliefs are equally true, in so doing we end up sacrificing truth itself.

Limiting your options

'If something can't be discovered by science, then it is not worth knowing,' stated one student after a talk that I gave. Popular as this view is, does it actually make sense? Can the statement itself be shown to be true scientifically? In chapter 2 we will look at the value of science in discovering truth. But we'll also see that other disciplines can help us find truth. That is why in this book we will not only look at arguments from science, but also from philosophy, psychology, sociology, archaeology and history.

There is another danger: that we limit our questions about truth to the lecture theatre, and detach them from real life. Do my beliefs make sense of life? Can I live consistently with them? C. S. Lewis explained, 'I believe in Christianity as I believe that the sun has risen: not only because I see it, but because by it I see everything else.'[3] We all need to ask, 'How do our beliefs make sense of our experiences of life? What kind of explanation do they give for the things that matter most to us? Can they satisfactorily explain my love of beauty and goodness, or my repulsion at evil? Do they explain why relationships are so important to us?'

Distractions

Around 350 years ago the French mathematician Blaise Pascal warned of the dangers of being so distracted that we don't consider the really important questions of life, and argued that these distractions 'lead us imperceptibly towards destruction'.[4] One of the reasons why we seek distraction is that thinking about reality can be uncomfortable. It is much easier to watch a comedy than to watch the news.

If this was an issue in the seventeenth century, then how much more should we be wary of it today, with the even greater range of distractions available to us? With a smartphone in our pocket, there is no reason ever to be bored (at least until the battery dies at lunchtime). Even today I found myself on Facebook, watching a video of a dancing dog when I should have been writing this! Yet it is actually when we *are* bored that we might start to think about things that really matter. In fact, we need to give ourselves space to think. This is not always easy, nor is it comfortable, but it is definitely worth it if we want to discover the truth.

The greatest obstacle to truth

We've seen some of the cultural barriers to discovering truth. However, could the biggest hindrance actually be ourselves? The renowned physicist Richard Feynman said this in his 1974 commencement speech at the California Institute of Technology: 'The first principle is that you must not fool yourself – and you are the easiest person to fool . . . After you've not fooled yourself, it's easy not to fool other scientists.'[5] Danish philosopher Søren Kierkegaard similarly warned, 'Of all deceivers, fear most yourself.'[6] Many of us are quick to be suspicious of others. Perhaps you are suspicious of me: why am I writing this book? It is much harder to have a healthy suspicion of yourself.

When it comes to looking at evidence, most of us like to think that we are a bit like Sherlock Holmes or Hercule Poirot. We dispassionately weigh up the evidence and go wherever it leads. Other people may be biased . . . but not us! Is that really the case? Are we as open to the truth as we might think?

In his book *Thinking, Fast and Slow*,[7] Daniel Kahneman explains how our decision-making process is more flawed than we might think. Kahneman won the Nobel Prize for his work on economic theory. He showed that investors can be blind to the biases of their own minds, and so they can make bad investment choices. The same principles also apply to us. We all have to decide what to believe, but we can be oblivious to our own biases in the process.

Kahneman explains that the reason for this is that we have two ways of thinking. Fast thinking is our intuitive sense of what is correct. Slow thinking is a more thorough process of thinking things through and weighing up the options. While slow thinking is more reliable, Kahneman shows that often we make decisions too fast, using only our intuition. This is because our minds are lazy – it takes effort to think things through deeply. Yet in not taking time to think properly, we can fall into a number of errors. For example:

- *Substituting a difficult question for an easy one.* In which car company should you invest your money? BMW or Peugeot? For many, that seems like an easy decision. They'll go for BMW. However, is that the right decision?

What they have done is substitute a difficult question (Which is a better investment?) for an easy one (Which type of car do I like?). But the actual question is not easy. To answer it, you would need to know something about each company, their economic policy and their future plans. But that would take a lot more effort!

- *Availability bias.* Who do you think is more likely to have an extramarital affair – a politician or a doctor? Most people think it would be a politician, but the reality is that both are just as likely. So why do we think the way we do? Simply because the affairs of politicians are more widely reported than those of doctors. People often feel more unsafe on an aeroplane than in a car. In reality, the most dangerous part of the journey is always on the road to the airport. Airline disasters always make the headlines; car crashes don't.

- *Confirmation bias.* I have sometimes listened to my more 'geeky' friends debate the relative benefits of certain types of smartphone. The funny thing is that they almost always think that the phone they own is the best one, and that the others are rubbish! Why? Because when we have invested our money in buying something, we are more likely to overestimate its positive features and overlook its shortcomings. We want to convince ourselves that we have made the right decision, so we struggle to look at the evidence impartially.

Are Christians biased?

Such flaws don't just affect how we invest our money. They can also affect what we choose to believe. For instance, it's easy to see how a Christian could be biased in his or her own assessment of the evidence for God. When asking, 'Does God exist?' they could simply substitute this for an easier question:

'What do I think of Christians?' My positive emotional experience of the Christian community could sway my thinking. A Christian could also be guilty of 'availability bias'. By surrounding himself with other Christians, by only reading Christian books and by only listening to Christian speakers, it could appear that his case is overwhelmingly strong. Yet he may not have exposed himself to arguments presenting another way.

Similarly, a Christian will be susceptible to 'confirmation bias' once he is publicly known for what he believes. He's staked not just his money, but also his life, on his beliefs. It would be easy for him to be blind to potential problems, and only see those things that appear to confirm his belief. In his book *Tricks of the Mind*, illusionist Derren Brown explains, 'This is the fallacy of the True Believer. The True Believer is impervious to real-world evidence because he just ignores anything that doesn't fit his belief system. Instead, he notices everything that matches and supports his beliefs . . .'[8]

We can all be biased

However, is it only the Christian who can be guilty of such flaws? Couldn't those with opposing beliefs also do the same? Kahneman points out, 'It is much easier, as well as more enjoyable, to identify and label the mistakes of others, than to recognize our own.'[9]

How might this work the other way? First, just as a Christian's positive experience of the church could bias them in favour of belief in God, so a negative experience of the church could send a person in the opposite direction. When someone says, 'I don't believe God exists', it might not be a rational decision, made after careful investigation of the evidence. It could be an emotional reaction to a painful past experience.

They could also all be susceptible to 'availability bias'. Is it possible to make a reasoned decision if you *only* read books by people who agree with you and who share your current beliefs? I would suggest that, given the current intellectual climate in the Western world, an atheist is possibly more prone to this bias than is a Christian. It is very rare to hear a reasoned defence of Christianity in the popular media. It is not that such a thing does not exist, but it is very unlikely to get exposure.

Finally, just as a Christian can be guilty of 'confirmation bias', the same could be said of the atheist, or, indeed, the Muslim, Hindu or the one with whatever belief he has. This will be the case especially if we are publicly known for our beliefs, or if our family or friends share the same beliefs. We will be much more likely to give weight to things that confirm our beliefs than to things that challenge them.

So is it possible to know the truth?

If we are all so susceptible to such biases, it may be tempting to ask, 'Is it possible for any of us really to know the truth?'

While understandable, such scepticism is unnecessary. Kahneman's point is not that we are incapable of making good decisions – we aren't – but to do so, we need to be aware of our own biases. We also need to be prepared to use our brains; for big and important questions, we cannot rely on our intuition alone. We need to slow down and think things through, and that will take some effort, as Kahneman observes: 'Questioning what we believe and want is difficult at the best of times, and especially difficult when we most need to do it, but we can benefit from the informed opinions of others.'[10]

It is in this vein that I hope this book will be of benefit to you.

Further reading

To help you to know where to turn to investigate these issues in greater depth, I have rated the further reading:

❯ Mild – a popular-level introduction to the subject that can be enjoyed with a glass of wine

❯❯ Medium – a more in-depth academic work that will require more effort to digest

❯❯❯ Hot – a more technical work requiring full brain engagement. Best read with a strong coffee!

❯ Os Guinness, *Time for Truth: Living Free in a World of Lies, Hype and Spin* (Baker, 2000)

❯❯ Paul Copan, *'True for You, But Not for Me': Overcoming Objections to Christian Faith*, 2nd revd edn (Bethany House Publishers, 2009)

❯❯❯ Douglas R. Groothuis, *Truth Decay: Defending Christianity against the Challenges of Postmodernism* (IVP, 2000)

1. BUT ISN'T FAITH IRRATIONAL?

Recently I was getting my hair cut. If you've seen the photo of me on the back cover, you'll realize that this process doesn't take very long. But a 'four' on top and 'two' on the sides is still long enough to have a significant conversation. On this particular occasion the woman cutting my hair was new, so we began (where many conversations do) by talking about our respective jobs. After she discovered my profession, we had a fascinating discussion about God. After a while she looked at me in the mirror and said, 'I really admire your faith.'

I was slightly taken aback by the unexpected compliment. She hadn't admired my *face*, but I thought that admiring my *faith* still wasn't bad. I thought for a second about how to respond and then asked, 'What do you think faith is?'

She stopped cutting for a moment, and then responded, completely seriously and without sarcasm, 'Faith is believing what you know isn't true!'

I looked up at her in the mirror and asked, 'Are you sure

you admire that? I mean, I think I'd pity someone with that kind of ability!'

For many people, faith is just that – an ability to believe things that are not true (though it is not always stated quite so bluntly). We can think that some people may have been born with some special ability for such foolishness, but most of us are glad not to be one of them. Isn't faith what you need when there is no evidence?

That is what Oxford professor Richard Dawkins thinks. He states, 'Faith is belief in spite of, even perhaps because of, the lack of evidence.'[1] He asserts, 'Faith . . . demands a positive suspension of critical faculties.'[2]

The atheist philosopher A. C. Grayling agrees: 'Faith is a commitment to belief contrary to evidence and reason . . . to believe something in the face of evidence and against reason – to believe something by faith – is ignoble, irresponsible and ignorant, and merits the opposite of respect.'[3]

Or, slightly more amusingly, Mark Twain put it this way: 'Faith is believing what you know ain't so.'[4]

So, it seems that you are presented with a choice. Either you are a person of faith *or* a person of reason. You either value rational thinking and evidence, *or* you are foolish, gullible and believe things that have no evidence – such as God, Jesus or the flying spaghetti monster. Faith may be practised by the young or gullible, but shouldn't the rest of us have grown out of it, just as we have done with our belief in Santa Claus and fairy tales?

What is faith?

We have seen that when people talk of faith, it is often a faith 'in spite of' the evidence. Of course, if we define faith in this way, it is not surprising that it then gets rejected as irrational.

However, is that definition of faith consistent with the way we use the word in any other context?

- A wife can 'have faith in' her husband, or a child in his parents. We can 'have faith in' our friends.
- I 'have faith' every time I go flying. I literally trust my life to the aircraft and the pilot, and I have good reasons to do so (even when I paid only 99p for the ticket!).
- Whenever I drive to a new location, I place a significant amount of 'faith' in my satnav to tell me the right way to go. It's not 100% accurate – it once tried to take me through the middle of a river – but it is sufficiently reliable that I will normally follow its directions.

Faith in all these cases is trust based *upon* evidence. Faith here is not in spite of the evidence, but because of it. You can have reasons for trusting a spouse, a friend, even an airline pilot or a satnav!

We can also 'lose faith' in people or organizations. When we do, it is again based on assessing evidence.

- A wife may 'lose faith in' her husband if the evidence of an affair comes to light.
- When I considered flying with Air Malawi, I had second thoughts when I discovered that someone, frustrated by their frequent unscheduled stops, had amusingly renamed them 'Air WhereAreWe?' On the basis of the evidence available, I decided it might be better to go with another airline.
- I 'lost my faith in' the new Maps App on my phone when it repeatedly took me to the wrong place.

There are many instances where we can see that faith is reasonable. It is impossible to live life without exercising faith of some sort, even though we may not consider it a 'religious faith'. Indeed, we could not begin to study science (or even do science) if we did not have faith in the work of other scientists, and trust that they have reported their findings truthfully.

We all have faith in different things, and normally this is not considered irrational at all.

But isn't Christian faith different?

So, is the problem not with faith in general, but with religious faith in particular? Isn't religious faith unfounded and lacking good reasons? Isn't it a bit like believing in an English summer where it doesn't rain, or in AFC Bournemouth winning the Champions League? Isn't it just wishful thinking?

My concern here is not to try to defend the rationality of all religious beliefs in general. In fact, I don't believe that all faiths are equally rational, or based on evidence. We may also want to question what some people regard as 'evidence'. Our purpose here is to see if there is a rational basis to Christianity. Is it a belief without evidence?

A. C. Grayling certainly thinks so. He believes that Jesus himself commends this type of faith in one of the stories in the Gospels. At the end of John's Gospel we are told that Thomas was not present when Jesus showed himself to be risen from the dead. Despite the repeated testimony of his friends, he refused to believe. It wasn't until a week later, when Thomas himself physically met the resurrected Jesus, that he finally believed. Jesus then said to Thomas, 'Because you have seen me, you have believed; blessed are those who have not seen and yet have believed.'[5] Doesn't that show that even Jesus thought that faith was without reason?[6]

Yet notice that Jesus is not contrasting faith and *reason*, but faith and *sight*! These are quite obviously different. I may believe in something I cannot visually see, yet still have a very good reason for doing so. If my beliefs are limited to what I have *personally* observed, then it would be very hard to believe much at all! I've never seen Napoleon, but I believe he lived; similarly, I've never seen electricity, but every day I rely on its effects to write this book.

What is more, when you read the context of the verse in question (a good thing to do with any verse from the Bible), you can see this even more clearly. The very next verse goes on to say, 'Jesus performed many other signs in the presence of his disciples, which are not recorded in this book. But these are written that you may believe that Jesus is the Messiah, the Son of God, and that by believing you may have life in his name.'[7]

The Gospel writer is not commending faith without reason. In fact, the reason why he wrote the Gospel was to give people reasons for believing! Of course, that may raise many questions about whether you can trust the Gospels, and we'll look at this in chapters 7 and 8. For now, it is enough to realize that Jesus is simply not commending irrational faith. Elsewhere in the same Gospel Jesus is recorded as saying, 'Believe me when I say that I am in the Father and the Father is in me; or at least believe on the evidence of the works themselves.'[8] Jesus is not asking people to believe without evidence.

This idea of faith being opposed to reason is quite alien in the New Testament (the second part of the Bible written after Jesus). The Greek word that is translated as 'faith' is the slightly rude-sounding *pistis*. This derives from a word meaning 'to be persuaded or convinced that something is

This idea of faith being opposed to reason is quite alien in the New Testament.

true'. One of the authors of part of the New Testament writes, 'For we did not follow cleverly devised stories . . . but we were eye-witnesses of his majesty.'[9]

The first Christians were eager to explain that their faith was reasonable. The book of Acts in the Bible documents the growth of Christianity in the first century, from its beginning in Jerusalem, all the way to Rome – the centre of the Empire. Along the way we find them 'debating', 'reasoning' and 'persuading' people – both in Jewish religious centres like Jerusalem, and also in the lecture rooms as in Ephesus and in the academic debating venues of cities such as Athens. The early Christians were convinced that their faith was true, not just personally true for them, but publicly true for everyone. They were convinced it would stand up to public debate.

On one occasion a Christian leader named Paul was on trial before a king called Agrippa and a Roman governor, Festus. During his defence Paul explained how he himself had not believed until he met Jesus, in a powerfully convincing and life-changing encounter. All this led Festus to butt in and tell Paul he was 'off his head'. Paul's response was measured and calm. He replied, 'I am not insane, most excellent Festus . . . What I am saying is true and reasonable. The king is familiar with these things, and I can speak freely to him. I am convinced that none of this has escaped his notice, because it was not done in a corner.'[10] Paul was convinced that the Christian claim would stand up to honest scrutiny, and that, for anyone having scrutinized it, the reasonable option would be to believe it, whoever they were – a slave, a king or a Roman governor. So, for the early Christians, faith was not an irrational belief in made-up stories, but the reasonable response to what they had heard and seen. Christian faith did not bypass the mind, but came through it.

It would appear, then, that the mistake made by many is that they define faith in a way that Christians have never done, and then reject it on that basis.[11] Francis Collins, an accomplished scientist and director of the Human Genome Project, says that the way many atheists define faith today 'certainly does not describe the faith of most serious believers in history, nor of most of those of my personal acquaintance'.[12] Faith is not the problem. So what is?

The problem of fundamentalism

There are obviously some Christians who have thought very little about the evidence for their faith. When challenged, they may simply respond by saying, 'I know what I believe – I don't need to look at the evidence.' The issue with such an attitude is that no matter what you say, you couldn't shake their faith, because it is not something they think about. They don't engage with questions, but sweep them under the carpet, confident that what they believe *must* be true. Such an attitude could be described as that of a fundamentalist, that is, a person who holds their beliefs very strongly but is unwilling to engage seriously with those who think otherwise. Such an attitude might give the impression that one's faith is strong, but actually the reality is the opposite. It is when I am insecure and uncertain in my beliefs that I would shy away from discussing them with those who disagree.

While there are some Christians who come into this category, it would be a mistake to think of this as the 'normal' or 'majority' Christian position. Most Christians are willing to engage with those who don't believe, and should be able to 'give a reason'[13] for what they believe, as the Bible actually says they should be able to do.

For my own part, I am very thankful that, as a child, my Christian parents encouraged me to engage with questions, and find my own reasons for what I believed. Growing up in Leicester, the first city in Britain to have an 'ethnic majority', I had many opportunities to discuss things with people with many different worldviews. This continues today. In the last ten years I have travelled around the university campuses of Europe, dialoguing with those who don't believe in God, and who are eager to tell me why. I try to make sure that I never give a talk without offering a chance for a public 'question-and-answer' session afterwards, and I will often devote as much time to taking questions as I will to giving the talk itself.

It is also worth remembering that it is not just Christians who can fall into fundamentalism. Anyone can, including an atheist. In fact, the scientist Peter Higgs accuses Richard Dawkins of doing exactly that. Speaking shortly after the discovery of the Higgs particle[14] at CERN in 2012, Higgs (not a Christian himself) said, 'Fundamentalism is another problem. I mean, Dawkins in a way is almost a fundamentalist himself, of another kind.' Why? Because on this topic, rather than engage with other academics and respected scholars, he 'concentrate[s] his attack on fundamentalists. But there are many believers who are just not fundamentalists . . .'[15]

It was a question I put to Dawkins on Twitter, after he reposted a tweet commending a video of a discussion between himself and the Christian theologian and apologist Alister McGrath. The video was an out-take from the TV documentary *The Root of All Evil*. I tweeted in response: 'I've always wondered why this one wasn't broadcast? Was it because it was too polite and reasonable?'

To his credit, Dawkins did respond:

Richard Dawkins @RichardDawkins · 28 Mar 2013
Fair cop, I do attack the extremes. But I'm truly curious: setting aside the
extremes, why does anyone believe even MODERATE religion? Why?

RETWEETS FAVORITES
115   90

11:48 AM · 28 Mar 2013 · Details

It's fine to attack the extremes, just don't give the impression
that they are the only people out there! But if he wants to
know why people believe in 'moderate religion', then maybe
he should talk with more reasonable people and fewer
extremists.

There are plenty of Christians (and atheists too) who are
not fundamentalists, and are willing to engage seriously with
those who disagree with them and look at the best arguments
against what they believe. Christianity, if true, has nothing to
fear from good honest questions. The secular philosopher
John Gray observed that, in his opinion, it is often believers,
not the New Atheists, who are more open to reasoned
dialogue: 'One cannot engage in dialogue with religious
thinkers in Britain today without quickly discovering that
they are, on the whole, more intelligent, better educated and
strikingly more freethinking than unbelievers (as evangelical
atheists still incongruously describe themselves).'[16]

But can you prove it?

We have seen that Christian faith is not opposed to reason.
But does that mean it's true? 'You can't prove Christianity' is
something I am regularly told, and that is correct. However,
there are many things that we can't prove 100%, and yet we
still believe them. It does not mean that those things are
irrational or unreasonable. Strictly speaking, 'proof' is found
in very few disciplines, even in the natural sciences. Rather,

we talk about probability or degrees of confidence. Some things are more reasonable than others, and just because you can't be 100% sure, it doesn't mean you can't make a reasonable decision.

For instance, imagine your local football team is top of the Premiership (now, that may take a lot of imagination for some, including myself!). They are seven points clear, with two games to go. You'd think that with only another six points available to everyone, they are sure to win the title? Well, not quite. Just imagine that, a day before the final game, the club is shown to have financial irregularities, and they go into administration and are docked ten points. Gutted! Suddenly you're off top spot. So, does the lack of absolute certainty mean you shouldn't celebrate? Of course not! The chances of that scenario happening are very small, so the reasonable thing to do would be to enjoy being champions. However, such an attitude would be very unreasonable if you still had half the season to go – you may still win, but it is much less certain!

Forgive me if you don't like football, but the point is this: 100% probability is not something we have very often, but that doesn't stop us operating on what is reasonable. This book will not, and cannot, prove that Christianity is true, but it is my aim to show that there are good reasons to believe it, and, given the evidence, that it is more reasonable to believe it than to reject it.

It is also important to remember that, at its centre, Christianity is not about a theory to be proved, but about a person to be met, and you don't prove a person. However, you *can* learn to *trust* them. And to trust someone, you need to get to know them. So, as well as looking at the evidence for Christianity, we will also seek to get to know the central character. We'll do this especially in the second half of the book.

Finally, you may wonder why faith is even required, if there is actually good evidence for something. If the evidence is so convincing, then surely you can just 'know' it – you don't need to 'believe' it? I would not talk about my faith in cows. I simply know that they exist. However, while faith has reasons, it also has consequences. To place my faith in something or someone indicates that, to some extent, I am trusting them, and that my faith has consequences for my life. Cows don't make a big difference to my life. However, if I am doing a tandem parachute jump, I am placing a great degree of faith in my instructor. There is much at stake! That is why, when it comes to the biggest questions of life, death and eternity, faith is required. Not because the evidence is small, but because the stakes are huge.

More than just rational

There is a danger in speaking about the rationality of the Christian faith. We can get so caught up with its rationality that we forget that it is not just true, but also wonderful. Let me illustrate: imagine there is a shy and rather geeky guy called Bill. One day he meets the woman of his dreams, except he is not dreaming – this is for real! What is more, contrary to Bill's expectations, she falls in love with him, and they get married. Bill would now have evidence, not least a wedding ring, to show her commitment to him, but, for Bill, her love for him would not be *merely* rational – it would be wonderful. He would pinch himself every morning and ask himself whether it could be true.

Similarly, Christianity reveals something about God that we would not have dared imagine by ourselves, and would scarcely have believed could be true. It tells us that, against all the odds, and in spite of how we have treated him, God has not written us off. In his love, he has made a way for us to restore our connection with him.

But before we get ahead of ourselves, we have to ask, 'How can the Christian faith be rational, when science has buried God?'

Further reading

❭ John C. Lennox, *Gunning for God: Why the New Atheists Are Missing the Target* (Lion Books, 2011)

❭ Alister McGrath, *Doubt in Perspective* (IVP, 2006)

❭❭ Kelly James Clark, *Return to Reason: A Critique of Enlightenment Evidentialism and a Defense of Reason and Belief in God* (Eerdmans, 1990)

❭❭ William Lane Craig, *Reasonable Faith: Christian Truth and Apologetics*, 3rd edn (Crossway, 2008)

❭❭ Francis A. Schaeffer, *Escape from Reason* (IVP, 2007)

❭❭❭ David Bentley Hart, *Atheist Delusions: The Christian Revolution and Its Fashionable Enemies* (Yale University Press, 2010)

❭❭❭ Dominic Erdozain, *The Soul of Doubt: The Religious Roots of Unbelief* (OUP USA, 2015)

❭❭❭ Alvin Plantinga, *Warranted Christian Belief* (OUP USA, 2000)

❭❭❭ Marilynne Robinson, *The Death of Adam: Essays on Modern Thought* (Picador USA, 2007)

❭❭❭ Richard Swinburne, *Faith and Reason*, 2nd edn (OUP USA, 2005)

2. BUT HASN'T SCIENCE BURIED GOD?

I was recently in discussion with an atheist in the small but beautiful country of Montenegro. We were preparing for a public debate where we were both going to be speaking later that day. I noticed that while he was normally very relaxed and quiet, when we got on to the topic of God, he suddenly became much more animated. I asked him why he was so passionate about it. (There are lots of things that I don't believe in, but I don't get worked up about them in the same way.)

'I'm motivated by truth,' he began, 'nothing else. I'm a scientist, and I want to have a society which is not dogmatic, for dogma is dangerous,' he asserted (ironically, somewhat dogmatically).

A few weeks beforehand I had been speaking at a series of events organized by Christian students at the Kiev Polytechnic Institute in Ukraine. As we invited people to the events, we often encountered the same rejection – 'Sorry, I'm a scientist!'

For many, like Professor Peter Atkins, it would appear that science and faith are mutually exclusive: 'Science and religion cannot be reconciled . . .' he states. 'Religion has failed and its failures should stand exposed. Science . . . should be acknowledged as king.'[1]

So, has science buried God? Has he inevitably been discarded in the face of scientific advancement? For some, like the students I met in Kiev, science is the only reason needed to dismiss God. Others may be more positive about the idea of God's existence, but wonder how such an idea can fit with their scientific study. Must we keep them apart as we would do with fighting children? Do we have to end up living in two different worlds – the world of science and the world of faith?

The origins of science

There is something rather strange and even ironic about this apparent conflict between God and science. For the modern study of science didn't grow out of an atheistic worldview. Quite the opposite – the science we know today is strongly rooted in the three Abrahamic faiths: Judaism, Christianity and Islam. Now it is often claimed that there were no other worldviews that it *could* have come from back then. Yet, while this may have been broadly true in the West, it certainly wasn't the case universally. Why didn't science grow similarly out of the polytheistic or pantheistic worldviews of other parts of the world? Historians of science agree that it was not accidental that the study of science grew where it did. Why?

It was because, in the West, there was the belief that nature was a real and good thing, created by God, but distinct from him. This provided the philosophical basis to do science. If, by contrast, we think that nature is an illusion, we won't study it. Similarly, if we think nature is god, then we wouldn't necessarily investigate it, but just worship it.

C. S. Lewis explained it well when he said, 'Men became scientific because they expected Law in nature, and they expected Law in nature because they believed in a Legislator.' He continues, 'In most modern scientists this belief has died: it will be interesting to see how long their confidence in uniformity survives it.'[2]

Francis Bacon, often described as 'the father of modern science', believed that God had given humanity two books: the book of nature and the Bible, and that we should study both. In reading the Bible they were studying the *words* of God, but in doing science they were studying his *works*.

Many of the early scientists were firm believers. Among them were Boyle, Kepler, Newton, Galileo, Faraday and Kelvin. Far from seeing their belief in God as a hindrance to their science, they saw it as their motivation. Kepler explained, 'I had the intention of becoming a theologian, but now I see how God is, by my endeavours, also glorified in astronomy, for "the heavens declare the glory of God".'[3]

Recently I delivered a series of talks in Cambridge at Great St Mary's, the University Church. The first talk was on this very subject. Interestingly, the church was also the location where the famous astronomer Sir Fred Hoyle gave one of a series of lectures in 1957 in which he decried the 'dogma of religion' in favour of the 'rational thinking' of science. On my way to the church I passed by the old Cavendish Laboratories where Watson and Crick discovered the double helix structure of DNA. Inscribed above the doors are words from the Bible:

Great are the works of the LORD;
    they are pondered by all who delight in them.[4]

Many of the pioneers of science would find it quite strange to hear about a 'conflict between science and faith'!

Why are science and God seen as enemies?

So, if the modern study of science grew out of Christianity, where did the idea of a conflict come from? Why do so many people today think that we must choose between science and God? There are a number of possible reasons.

- People often think of historical examples, like in the case of Galileo. He challenged the wrongly, yet widely, held belief that our world is at the centre of the universe. The church's reported persecution of Galileo is seen as an example of this ongoing conflict.
- The apparent conflict between science and God is not confined to historical cases; it certainly seems to be very much an issue today. It is perhaps not surprising that we may think this, given the frequency with which high-profile atheist scientists appear in the media. Those such as Richard Dawkins and Brian Cox enjoy a significant amount of airtime here in the UK, and this can give the impression that nearly all scientists are atheists – a view that Richard Dawkins himself suggests is borne out by the evidence. He cites a survey that found that 95% of leading scientists in America are atheists.[5]
- God is often seen as a 'God of the gaps'. This is the idea that God only exists as an explanation to fill the gaps in our scientific knowledge. Richard Dawkins sums up this position well when he sarcastically says, 'If you don't understand how something works, never mind: just give up and say God did it. You don't know how the nerve impulse works? Good! You don't understand how memories are laid down in the brain? Excellent! Is photosynthesis a bafflingly complex process? Wonderful! Please don't go to work on the problem,

just give up, and appeal to God.'[6] If God were just a 'God of the gaps', then it would make sense for God and science to be opposed. For, in that case, the more that science explained, the less we would need God. The need for a 'God of the gaps' is inversely proportional to our understanding of science. Belief in such a God would certainly diminish our desire to investigate the world.

• Possibly the biggest reason for this apparent conflict is the theory of evolution. In the minds of many it was Darwin who put the final nail in God's coffin. Not only does evolution appear to contradict particular understandings of design in nature; it also seems to tell a different story from the opening chapters of the Bible. According to some people, this reinforces the idea that you have to choose between what science tells us and what the Bible teaches.

What are we to make of these claims? Has science finally got rid of our need for God . . . or has his obituary been written somewhat prematurely? Let's look at each of the above reasons in turn.

Have science and God always been in conflict?

The belief that science and faith have always been in conflict is a very popular notion, but is it actually true? Colin Russell, formerly Professor of the History of Science at the Open University, said it 'is not only historically inaccurate, it is a caricature so grotesque that what needs to be explained is how it could have possibly achieved any degree of respectability'.[7] Indeed, how *did* this idea of conflict emerge?

Perhaps most significant was the publication of two books in the nineteenth century: *History of the Conflict between Religion and Science* by John Draper and *History of the Warfare of Science with Theology in Christendom* by Andrew White.[8] You can tell from the titles that there is to be no mistaking the authors' main ideas.

While very few people today have actually heard of these books, it's amazing how frequently the ideas within them are regurgitated; for instance, the idea that all Christians used to believe in a flat earth. The problem with many such claims is that they are highly selective – misrepresentations of history that use the exceptions to prove the norm.[9] Yet it is often the case that a lie will get halfway around the world before truth has put his shoes on! And this is especially true when the 'lie' in question is one that many people would *like* to believe.

There are some fundamental difficulties with this idea of an ongoing conflict through history between science and religion. For a start, how do we define science and religion? Using 'science' as an umbrella term for a number of different disciplines is a relatively recent thing. There may have been conflicts between individuals and groups, but they weren't between science and religion. This would be as fallacious as claiming that there has been conflict between the states of Israel and Egypt for the last 1,000 years – both have not even existed as states during most of that time.[10] In fact, it turns out that even the most popular stories of conflict, such as Galileo being persecuted by the church, were, in reality, quite different from the way they were portrayed.[11]

Writing in the *Cambridge Companion to Science and Religion*, Peter Harrison, one of the world's leading historians in this field, explains that while the conflict story has been popular, 'it is now generally accepted by historians that this [is] erroneous . . . the historical record simply does not bear out this model of enduring warfare'.[12]

Doesn't science naturally lead to atheism?

We've already seen that, historically, science did not naturally lead to atheism. However, what about today? Certainly it can appear to do so, given the prevalence of atheistic scientists in the media in the UK. Perhaps, though, it could be that this is a convenient impression that the media would like to portray? After all, a picture of controversy is far more newsworthy and interesting!

It may be true that currently the *majority* of top scientists are atheists, but it is also worth remembering that the majority are also white and male. Yet it would be incredibly racist and sexist to say that science is incompatible with being an African or a female.

What is certainly *not* true is that *all* scientists today are atheists. There is a big difference between saying there are not *any* scientists who believe in God and not *many* scientists who believe in God. If belief in God were incompatible with science, then surely we should not expect to find *any*. In reality, there are numerous examples of Christians working in the sciences, including geneticist Francis Collins, astronomer Jennifer Wiseman, botanist Ghillean Prance, palaeontologist Mary Higby Schweitzer, astrophysicist David Wilkinson and theoretical physicist John Polkinghorne, to name just a few.

We can still ask, though, why does atheism seem to increase with scientific learning? Well, one important thing to remember is that 'correlation' is not the same as 'causation'. For example, there is a 100% correlation between people who breathe and people who die. But we wouldn't suggest for a minute that one is therefore the cause of the other. My mathematician father used to quote Mark Twain, who said, 'There are lies, damn lies, and then there are statistics!' We need to be careful not to read into the statistics something that isn't necessarily there.

Another study interestingly shows perhaps a more surprising trend. In 1916 a random selection of 1,000 scientists were asked whether they believed in a personal God who answered prayer.[13] Just over a third said yes, about the same number said no, and just under a third said they weren't sure; they were agnostic. In 1996 the experiment was repeated. You might expect that, after a century of scientific advancement, the prevalence of atheism would have risen dramatically. However, the results had hardly changed. It seems that, contrary to popular opinion, the growth of science hasn't destroyed belief in God. Sociologist Peter Berger goes further. He asserts that the hypothesis that we are becoming more secular just is not true. 'There are a couple of social scientists who hold onto that theory,' he says, 'which in a way I admire. I somehow admire people who maintain their views in the face of empirical evidence!'[14]

So, why doesn't an increase in scientific understanding lead to a decrease in faith?

Is God in the gaps?

One of the reasons why people may expect belief in God to decrease with the increase in scientific understanding is that they view God as a 'God of the gaps'. They believe that he exists only as an explanation for the things that we don't yet understand. Historically, this may have meant attributing such events as thunder and lightning to the gods having a raging 'domestic'! Stephen Hawking states, 'Ignorance of nature's ways led people in ancient times to invent gods . . .'[15] Of course, if God only exists to fill the gaps of our knowledge, then the more we know, the less we need God.

However, it is just not true to think that God always becomes the explanation for all the things we don't understand. For instance, until recently, we didn't know why holes formed in Swiss cheese, but I don't know of any religious believer who attributed this to God! Also, while the 'God of the gaps' idea may describe the gods of some belief systems, it has nothing to do with the God of the Bible. The 'God of the gaps' is located within the universe – as part of the creation. The Bible portrays God as standing outside the universe, and responsible for it all. Let me illustrate.

I remember distinctly the first time I ever used a Dyson Airblade™. It was a very exciting day! Conventional hand-dryers in public toilets are notorious for being totally ineffect-ive, but I had heard it claimed that an Airblade could dry my hands in ten seconds flat. I remember washing my hands twice to enjoy the novelty. Now imagine if, struggling to com-prehend how such a machine could work so well, I come up with an idea. Mr Dyson must be a little man who lives inside the Airblade! He waits for the sound of the flushing toilet and springs into action to blow on my hands. Imagine if I then take the Airblade apart and discover that, instead of there being a Mr Dyson inside, there is simply a lot of electronics. I now conclude that there is no need for Mr Dyson, for I can see how the machine works. Of course, it doesn't take a rocket scientist to see the problem with my belief. Understanding how the Airblade works does not remove the need for a designer to make it in the first place.

Understanding how the universe works in no way removes the need for a God who made it.

That would be to confuse the mechanism (how it works) with the cause (why it exists at all).

In the same way, understanding how the universe works in no way removes the need for a God who made it. You won't find God fully explained within the universe, just as you won't find Mr Dyson in his Airblade. He's not the God of the bits we don't understand, but rather he stands behind everything there is.

This certainly seems to have been the conviction of Isaac Newton. When he drew his conclusions about the law of gravity, he didn't conclude, 'Great! Now I don't need God to do it.' Instead, he wrote a book, *Principia Mathematica*, in which he wanted to persuade the thinking person to believe in God because of the wonder of the universe he had created. He stated, 'This most beautiful System of the Sun, Planets, and Comets could only proceed from the counsel and dominion of an intelligent and powerful being . . . This Being governs all things, not as the soul of the world, but as Lord over all.'[16]

Rather than being a threat to belief in God, our increased understanding of science can actually multiply our appreciation of him. As we understand more of both the magnitude and intricacy of the universe, we can appreciate more of what he has made.

Take a moment to take a sip from a glass of water. How many water molecules have you just drunk? In just a small sip of just 18 ml there would be 6×10^{23} water molecules of H_2O! To picture how many molecules that is, imagine that each one was laid out on a road in 1 mm^2 spaces. How big would that road have to be to fit them all on it? Not only so long that it would reach to the moon, but it would have to be four times as wide as it is long![17]

Or think of the vastness of the universe. It takes 1.5 seconds for light to travel from the moon to the earth. It takes 8.3 minutes for it to get here from the sun, but it would take 100,000 years for light to pass through our little galaxy, the Milky Way. And our galaxy is one of at least 100 billion!

It's hard not to be filled with a sense of awe and wonder when we ponder even fairly simple facts about our universe. For the Christian, a greater appreciation of the wonder of the universe naturally flows into worship of the God who made it.

Francis Collins put it this way: 'Scientists who do not have a personal faith in God also undoubtedly experience the exhilaration of discovery. But to have that joy of discovery, mixed together with the joy of worship, is truly a powerful moment for a Christian who is a scientist.'[18]

How can you believe in evolution and the Bible?

For many people the biggest barrier between science and God is evolution. On the surface it may appear that evolution and the first chapters of the Bible give contradictory accounts of our origins. Certainly, there are some Christians who would tell us that we have to choose between them – an idea that gets great support (for opposing reasons!) from some well-known atheists.

However, it is simply not the case that it has to be either/or. While some Christians believe that God created the world in six literal days, other Christians believe that God created the universe and used the process of evolution to accomplish his purposes – a view often described as 'theistic evolution'. Among the people who hold this view is Simon Conway Morris, Professor of Evolutionary Palaeobiology at Cambridge University, one of the most eminent evolutionary biologists in the world.

Yet how can this view square with what the early chapters of the Bible say about God creating the world in six days? Do we have to reject part of the Bible? Absolutely not! But we do need to understand the Bible and the way in which it was written. The Bible is a library of books and contains different literary genres. For instance, there is history (like in the Gospel accounts) and there is poetry (like in the book of Psalms). No-one complains that the psalmist is being unscientific when he describes 'the rivers clapping their hands',[19] for it is quite obvious that he is writing poetry. In the same way, Christians have never thought that Jesus was just a metaphorical idea, because the authors of the Gospels clearly claim to be writing history.

The question is this: in which literary genre are the early chapters of Genesis written? The honest answer is: we're not sure. One of the difficulties is that, compared to the rest of the Bible, these chapters are unique. It is not immediately obvious what genre they are. However, it seems that the intention of the author of Genesis was not primarily to explain the mechanism of creation, but rather God's relationship to it.[20]

So, have Christians just reinterpreted the Bible to fit with what science teaches? Again – not at all. It wasn't that every Christian believed in a literal six-day creation until Darwin brought out *The Origin of Species*. Even as far back as the fourth century the great Christian thinker Augustine suggested that the days of Genesis were not the literal days of one week. After all, he pointed out, how could there have already been day and night when the sun was not created until day four?

We don't have to choose between the Bible and what science tells us about the development of life on Earth. Indeed, many of my Christian friends hold strongly to an evolutionary view of the world *and* to the Bible as being God's revealed Word.[21] 'Either half of my colleagues are enormously stupid,' said palaeontologist Stephen Jay Gould, 'or else the science of Darwinism is fully compatible with conventional religious beliefs – and equally compatible with atheism.'[22] For Darwin himself, loss of faith doesn't appear to have had anything to do with his scientific work. In fact, his great American promoter Asa Gray was a devout non-conformist Christian.

So we don't have to choose between evolution and the Bible. Neither is it true that just because evolution can explain how biology has become complex, there is no intelligence behind the universe.

Imagine if you saw a car travelling down the road. It would be logical to assume that there was an intelligence that was responsible for its movement (and we would normally call such intelligence 'a driver'). However, imagine that this car is actually the driverless Google car. Do you now assume that there is no intelligence behind the movement of the car? Of course not! It takes even *more* intelligence to make a car that can drive itself.

Alternatively, I could introduce you to my friend Martin. He has the exciting job of designing robots. Martin's robots have a very specific purpose. They chop and stick bubble wrap padding into the bottom of fruit punnets. Chances are, if you've ever bought a punnet of strawberries in the UK, the wrap at the bottom was stuck in by one of Martin's robots! Now, which would take more intelligence – for Martin manually to stick each pad in every single punnet, or for him to design something that will do it for him?

Back in the time of Darwin, novelist Charles Kingsley put it this way: 'God is so wise he can make all things make themselves.' Darwin obviously appreciated his comments, for he cited them in the second edition of *The Origin of Species*.[23] If the complexity of evolution tells us something of the wonderful process by which God chose to create, perhaps that might make our view of God even bigger?

Could evolution be a bigger difficulty for atheists?

If evolution were *all* we had to explain who we are, then this would raise serious questions about all beliefs, atheism included. For the driving force behind evolution is the need for survival, *not* necessarily the need to perceive truth. Therefore, why should we trust that our brains have evolved to tell us what is true, rather than simply what is beneficial?

'That's a load of rubbish!' was the response of one student at the University of Bath when I explained this idea. 'Surely discerning truth *is* beneficial for our survival – wouldn't it be better to know that the animal in the distance is a tiger who might eat me, rather than a pussy cat that I could keep as pet?'

'Of course,' I responded. 'On a physical level, truth may be beneficial, but why should that always be the case, especially in the realm of metaphysics (ideas)?'[24]

He obviously wasn't convinced, and I wasn't sure what else I could say to try to explain things more clearly. I admitted as much, but told him that I would think about it some more and get back to him.

After a few days we happened to meet again in the corridor of the physics department. We got chatting, and I asked if I could try to explain better what I had meant before.

'Let me give you an example,' I began. 'The majority of the world's population believe in some kind of God . . .'

'That doesn't prove anything!' he butted in.

'Of course not,' I responded, 'but can you explain why it is that if there is no God, so many people believe in him?'

'Oh, that's easy!' he explained. 'There's a simple evolution-ary explanation as to why people become religious.'

'But isn't that exactly the issue?' I responded. 'You've just told me that evolution has caused people to believe things that you think aren't true! But how do you know that it hasn't also done the same for those who are atheists?'

Darwin himself expressed this doubt in one of his letters to a friend:

> But then with me the horrid doubt always arises whether the convictions of man's mind, which has been developed from the mind of the lower animals, are of any value or at all trustworthy. Would any one trust in the convictions of a monkey's mind, if there are any convictions in such a mind?[25]

Darwin himself was by no means an atheist, but many atheists have seen the issue too. John Gray, who was until recently Professor of the History of European Thought at the London School of Economics, writes, 'Modern humanism is the faith that through science humankind can know the truth and so be free. But if Darwin's theory of natural selection is true this is impossible. The human mind serves evolutionary success, not truth.'[26] Professor Thomas Nagel agrees: 'Evolutionary naturalism implies that we should not take any of our convictions seriously, including the scientific world picture on which evolutionary naturalism itself depends.'[27] Philosopher Alvin Plantinga has done extensive thinking on this idea, which he refers to as 'the evolutionary argument against naturalism'.[28]

This is not to say that atheists can't do good science. They can, and many of them plainly do. The question is *not*: 'Who can do the best science?' but rather: 'Which worldview provides the best foundation for doing science in the first place?' Many scientists have found that a worldview that starts with God provides the strongest foundation and the best reason. We shouldn't be at all surprised or embarrassed, then, to find Christians operating in the sciences.

So where does the problem lie?

I hope I have helped you to see that there is no conflict between science and God. So, where does the conflict lie? Not between God and science, but with what we may call 'scientism'. Scientism is a philosophical, rather than a truly scientific, position. It is the belief that science is the *only* way to know whether anything is true.

A clear example of this idea is found in the words of Bertrand Russell: 'Whatever knowledge is attainable must be attained by scientific methods, and what science cannot discover, mankind cannot know.'[29] Peter Atkins agrees when he says, 'There is no reason to suppose that science cannot deal with every aspect of existence.'[30] Stephen Hawking put it this way in his book *The Grand Design*: 'Philosophy is dead . . . Scientists have become the bearer of the torch of discovery in our quest for knowledge.'[31]

The irony of all these statements is that they are self-refuting. None of them are statements *of* science, but rather statements *about* science. There is no way scientifically to verify the statement that philosophy is dead. It is indeed a philosophical claim! It is true that not all great philosophers are great scientists, but this also shows that not all scientists are great philosophers.[32]

Another problem with this idea is that it assumes that science and religion are both trying to answer the same questions. Christianity is not primarily trying to explain the mechanisms of how certain things in the empirical world work. In the same way, science cannot and will not answer the big metaphysical questions such as: 'Why is there a universe at all?', 'What is the meaning of my life?', and 'What happens after we die?' Can science judge a poem simply by the meter of the rhythm, or a painting by analysing the chemicals in the paint?

Ludwig Wittgenstein was one of the most influential philosophers of the twentieth century. He concluded his seminal work *Tractatus Logico-Philosophicus* by stating, 'We feel that even if all possible scientific questions have been answered, the problems of life have still not been touched at all.'[33]

Scientism would also be problematic to put into practice. If science is the only way to discover truth, then we should close down not only the theology department in every university, but also the entirety of the arts and humanities departments as well!

The reality is that while science is great for discovering many things, there are some questions that lie outside of its realm. For instance, how could I use science to determine whether an event in history took place? Real historical events are unrepeatable, so I could hardly produce the same event again by repeated experiment. Historical investigation is what would be needed.

This is particularly important in the question of God's existence, for the claim the Bible makes is that the surest way God has revealed himself is in person, in history. To investigate that claim, we'll definitely need to use our brains, but it will be the discipline of history, and not science, that will help us more.

Science has not buried God. But could psychology and sociology pose serious challenges? Don't people just believe in God because they want him to exist? Isn't religious belief simply defined by your upbringing and culture?

Further reading

❭ Francis Collins, *The Language of God* (Simon & Schuster UK, 2007)
❭ John C. Lennox, *Gunning for God: Why the New Atheists Are Missing the Target* (Lion Books, 2011)

⟩ Alister McGrath, *The Dawkins Delusion?* (SPCK, 2007)

⟩⟩ Richard Hooykaas, *Religion and the Rise of Modern Science* (Scottish Academic Press, 1972)

⟩⟩ John C. Lennox, *God's Undertaker: Has Science Buried God?* (Lion Books, 2009)

⟩⟩ Tom McLeish, *Faith and Wisdom in Science* (OUP, 2014)

⟩⟩ John Polkinghorne, *Quarks, Chaos and Christianity: Questions to Science and Religion* (Crossroad, 2006)

⟩⟩ John H. Walton, *The Lost World of Genesis One: Ancient Cosmology and the Origins Debate* (IVP USA, 2009)

⟩⟩ John H. Walton, *The Lost World of Adam and Eve: Genesis 2–3 and the Human Origins Debate* (IVP USA, 2015)

⟩⟩⟩ Henri Blocher, *In the Beginning: The Opening Chapters of Genesis* (IVP, 1984)

⟩⟩⟩ Peter Harrison, *The Territories of Science and Religion* (University of Chicago Press, 2015)

⟩⟩⟩ Alister McGrath, *Inventing the Universe: Why We Can't Stop Talking about Science, Faith and God* (Hodder & Stoughton, 2015)

⟩⟩⟩ Alvin Plantinga, *Where the Conflict Really Lies: Science, Religion, and Naturalism* (OUP USA, 2012)

3. BUT COULDN'T FAITH JUST BE A PSYCHOLOGICAL CRUTCH OR A SOCIAL CONSTRUCT?

We have seen that, contrary to popular opinion, science hasn't buried God, but could psychology or sociology do so instead? Is faith just divine wish-fulfilment? Aren't our beliefs determined by our culture?

Arguing from psychology

In his film *The Invention of Lying*, Ricky Gervais demonstrates, quite amusingly, the idea that faith is just a psychological crutch. Gervais plays Mark, the lead character, who lives in a world where no-one can lie. No-one, that is, except Mark! When he discovers his unique ability, he has a lot of fun with it – including conning the bank into releasing cash he doesn't own and convincing attractive women to sleep with him. He also discovers that it can be used for better purposes, and he uses it to stop a friend from committing suicide.

However, when Mark's own mother has a heart attack, he discovers that she is filled with fear at the prospect of an 'eternal nothingness'. (In a world without lying there cannot, according to Gervais, be any religion.) Desperate to help, Mark decides to lie, and tell his mother that she will go to a happy place that will last forever. The idea brings great comfort to his mum, who soon afterwards dies in peace. The news of this idea soon spreads, and Mark is forced to explain to the gathered crowds outside the hospital how they too can get to the happy place. In an unsubtle reference to the Bible, he says that they have to follow ten rules to keep the 'man in the sky' happy. If they break more than three of them, then they're out!

The film's message is clear: Christianity isn't true, but simply an invention that gullible people have 'bought into' because it gives them an illusory sense of hope.

Of course, Ricky Gervais wasn't the first to come up with this idea. Back in the seventeenth century the philosopher Francis Bacon explained, 'For what a man had rather were true he more readily believes.'[1]

However, it was the nineteenth-century German philosopher Ludwig Feuerbach who first sought to articulate this argument. His idea was that 'God is the highest subjectivity of man abstracted from himself.'[2] In other words, God is just a projection of ourselves into the heavens.

While Feuerbach stated this, it was Sigmund Freud who sought to explain why it was so. He said that religious beliefs are 'illusions, fulfilment of the oldest, strongest, and most urgent wishes of mankind. Thus the benevolent rule of the divine Providence allays our fears of the dangers of life.'[3]

He suggested that as we grow up, we replace the protection of our own fathers with that of a divine father figure. God is nothing more than the projection of our human longings into the heavens.[4]

While many are now suspicious of some of Freud's conclusions, the idea that God is simply the creation of our thinking is still common today. Bruce Hood, Professor of Psychology at the University of Bristol, explains this idea in his book *Supersense: Why We Believe the Unbelievable*. He says that our minds are set 'naturally to infer structures and patterns in the world and to make sense of it by generating intuitive theories'.[5]

So, if religion is just wish-fulfilment and childhood superstition, shouldn't we then grow out of it? Illusionist and atheist Derren Brown certainly thinks so. Brown was a professing Christian during his teenage years, but looking back now he explains, 'I just believed because I had always done and because it had come to be a very important psychological crutch.'[6]

Arguing from sociology

Another argument against God comes from the discipline of sociology. 'Aren't our beliefs simply determined by the culture around us?' That's to say, if you were born in Saudi Arabia, you probably wouldn't be a Christian.

Richard Dawkins takes this idea further and seeks to explain it through the concept of memes. Just as genes are pieces of biological information that decide *what* we are (our biology), so memes, he says, are pieces of cultural information that determine *who* we are (our biography). It is claimed that memes pass on cultural ideas from one generation to the next, just as our genes pass on our biology.

In this way, religion can be seen as a virus, passed on like a common cold . . . except, in Dawkins's opinion, it is much more dangerous. 'Faith is one of the world's great evils, comparable to the smallpox virus, but harder to eradicate . . . And who, looking at Northern Ireland or the Middle East, can be confident that the brain virus of faith is not exceedingly dangerous?'[7]

This idea is also clear from a T-shirt design being sold by the Richard Dawkins Foundation. For just $25, and available in a variety of colours with an accompanying designer bag, it proclaims to the world, 'Religion – together we can find the cure.'

So, is faith just a form of wish-fulfilment or a virus of the mind? Let's look at some of the difficulties with such ideas. We will apply each of these to the arguments from psychology and sociology respectively.

The arguments 'cut both ways'

The idea that religion is wish-fulfilment can simply be turned around. Couldn't atheism also be the same? If Christians believe in God because they *want* him to exist, couldn't atheists *not* believe in God because they *don't* want him to exist?

Certainly, some atheists have been willing to admit that this is, at least partly, the case. Thomas Nagel explains in his book *The Last Word*,

> I want atheism to be true and am made uneasy by the fact that some of the most intelligent and well-informed people I know are religious believers. It isn't just that I don't believe in God and, naturally, hope that I'm right in my belief. It's that I hope there is no God! I don't want there to be a God; I don't want the universe to be like that.[8]

Aldous Huxley felt similarly: 'I had motive for not wanting the world to have a meaning; consequently I assumed that it had none . . . For myself, the philosophy of meaninglessness was essentially an instrument of liberation, sexual and political.'[9]

Atheism could be a way of breaking free from divine authority. As Fyodor Dostoevsky said, 'If God does not exist, then everything is permissible.'

I could also ask, if belief in God is a projection of my positive experience of my father, then could atheism be a rejection of a negative experience of the atheist's father? Interestingly, in his book *Faith of the Fatherless*, Christian psychologist Paul Vitz studies some of the most famous atheists of all time: Nietzsche, Hume, Russell, Hitler, Stalin, Mao Zedong, Sartre and others. He concludes, 'We find a weak, dead or abusive father in every case.'[10]

It's worth adding here that I don't believe that all atheists are reacting against their negative experiences of fathers, or desiring wish-fulfilment. However, we humans are much more than simply brains on legs. Our desires do affect our beliefs. I know well that salad is a healthier choice than pan-fried steak. I don't doubt the evidence . . . but I desire steak far more than I desire salad . . . and so I make my decision: it's rib-eye for me!

This attitude may be acceptable when applied to my choice of dinner. But it is far more serious when applied to the ultimate questions of life. There is a real danger that we will simply believe what we want to believe, regardless of the evidence, especially if the alternative is uncomfortable. We can willingly suppress the truth when we don't like the implications.

Christopher Nolan explores this idea in his brilliant film *Inception*. In the central scene, Cobb, the main character (Leonardo DiCaprio), is explaining to Ariadne, his young assistant, why his wife died: 'She's locked something away, something . . . something deep inside,' he whispers. 'A truth that she had once known but chose to forget.'[11]

'Most ignorance is vincible ignorance,' states Aldous Huxley. 'We don't know because we don't want to know. It is our will that decides upon what subjects we shall use our intelligence.'[12] Christian philosopher Douglas Groothuis agrees. He explains that while sometimes we yearn for truth, at other times we run from it: 'When truth unmasks and convicts us, and we refuse to return its gaze, we would rather banish it in favour of our own self-serving and protective version of reality.'[13] It is easy to see how other people might be susceptible to this. It is much harder for us to admit this in ourselves, but if we don't, then we will be blind to our own biases.

The argument from sociology also works in the other direction. If our beliefs are just determined by our culture, why should that only apply to the religious sphere? We could equally say, 'If you were born in Saudi Arabia, then you probably wouldn't be an atheist.' How do we know that our atheism isn't simply based on our culture? Certainly, in the West, since the Age of Enlightenment this has become a far more dominant concept. As a result, it is much easier to be an atheist than a Bible-believing Christian in most universities today. This should make us ask, 'Who is it that is simply copying the culture around them?'

The arguments from both psychology and sociology could just as easily be used against atheism as they could be for arguments supporting it. This should make us start to question whether they can help us discover what is actually true.

The idea undermines truth

If all our ideas and beliefs are tainted by our psychological state, then why not this idea as well? It is somewhat naive to claim that everyone else is influenced by their psychological state, but not us. How can we begin to claim such unique objectivity? We have to decide: if other people's ideas are prone to this, then so too must ours be. If our beliefs are not *totally* governed by our psychological state, then could this not also be the case for other people's beliefs too?

The same problem applies to the idea that religion is just a 'meme'. I was discussing the idea of memes in a philosophy class that I was leading. One of the women interrupted and asked, 'What's your problem with the concept of memes? Is it because you think it will undermine your Christianity?'

I responded, 'No, it's because if we are not careful, they undermine the very concept of truth, and your atheism as well. If religion is just a meme and nothing more than a meme, then why stop with religion? Couldn't all ideas be memes, atheism included? Indeed, the very idea of memes would itself be a meme!'

Another big problem with the idea of memes is that because the word sounds like 'genes', it can be assumed that they carry equal scientific weight. This could not be further from the truth. The now-closed *Journal of Memetics* concluded its final article by admitting that the concept 'had been a short-lived fad whose effect has been to obscure more than it has been to enlighten. I am afraid that memetics, as an identifiable discipline, will not be widely missed.'[14] Memes are a pseudoscience with serious ramifications.

When we assume that a belief is just a meme, then we can stop looking for reasons why people hold their beliefs, and we look instead for causes. It is one thing to say that our beliefs are influenced by our desires and our culture. It is quite another to say that they cause them. The minute we say that, all rational discussion goes out of the window. C. S. Lewis explained it using the analogy of a radio. We admit that the atmosphere can affect the quality of the sound. However, if we thought that the atmosphere was solely responsible for all of the sound, we would never bother to listen to the radio![15]

The concept of memetics is also dangerous. If you think that beliefs are caused rather than just influenced, then you stop interacting with other people rationally and respectfully. Instead, you just ridicule and deride those you disagree with. For some, this may take the form of patronizing T-shirts that claim you'll find a cure to religion! Self-styled 'street epistemologist' (think atheist evangelist) Peter Boghossian goes even further. He suggests that religious belief should be categorized as a psychiatric illness. He explains, 'We must reconceptualize faith as a virus of the mind, and treat faith like other epistemological crises: contain and eradicate.' He continues, 'There's also an urgent need for large-scale interventions in educational systems, houses of worship, and other institutions that promote failed epistemologies.'[16]

This idea that anyone who's not an atheist is not merely in disagreement but is dangerous, divisive or deluded has a chilling precedent. Soviet propaganda warned, 'Religion is poison: protect your children.' Within five years of the Russian Revolution 2,500 priests, 1,900 monks and 3,000 nuns had been executed. By 1940 the number of churches in the country had been reduced from 54,000 to just a few hundred.[17] Before we adopt an idea, we would do well to consider the potential consequences. Atheistic ideas have not always been as benign as many contemporary bloggers would like us to believe.

All our desires cannot be wrong

If desiring something to be true means that it cannot be so, this would lead to some rather huge difficulties. For instance, it would be impossible for all the desires of everyone to be simultaneously false! At least some of our desires must relate to truth. Indeed, we find that some of our desires do relate to reality, as C. S. Lewis explained:

The Christian says, 'Creatures are not born with desires unless satisfaction for those desires exists. A baby feels hunger: well, there is such a thing as food. A duckling wants to swim: well, there is such a thing as water. Men feel sexual desire: well, there is such a thing as sex. If I find in myself a desire which no experience in this world can satisfy, the most probable explanation is that I was made for another world.'[18]

If God does exist, then should it surprise us that we were made with a desire for him? That is, in fact, exactly what the Bible claims. 'He has set eternity in the human heart'[19] is the way one of the Old Testament writers put it. This has also been the experience of many throughout history. Augustine said, 'Our hearts are restless until they find their rest in you.'[20] Pascal, the French mathematician whom we met earlier, reflected,

What else does this craving, and this helplessness, proclaim but that there was once in man a true happiness, of which all that now remains is the empty print and trace? This he tries in vain to fill with everything around him, seeking in things that are not there the help he cannot find in those that are, though none can help, since this infinite abyss can be filled only with an infinite and immutable object; in other words by God himself.[21]

Could our desires actually be a pointer to a God who really is there and desires to be known by us?

Could our desires actually be a pointer to a God who really is there and desires to be known by us?

The idea is not borne out in reality

The idea that Christianity is just a wish-fulfilment or the product of our culture does not square with reality. The evidence suggests something quite different.

If Christianity is just a psychological crutch for weak people, then you would expect only weak, vulnerable and gullible people to believe it, but there are plenty of people who don't fit into these categories at all, and yet who follow Jesus Christ. And for many, believing in Jesus hasn't made things easier, but harder.

For the first Christians, belief normally meant rejection, persecution and very often death. The same is true for many Christians today. Occasionally, the world's media report such abuses: there was a horrified reaction to the case of Meriam Ibrahim, a Sudanese Christian, who refused to renounce her faith despite being chained throughout her pregnancy and continually threatened with execution. Thankfully, she was eventually released and able to flee the country. There was no such opportunity for the 147 students gunned down early one morning at their university in Garissa, Kenya, because of their belief in Jesus. These are the few cases that do make it into the popular press; most incidents go unreported.

Recently, *The Independent* newspaper bucked that trend by running an article entitled 'Christians: The world's most persecuted people'.[22] It reported that according to the International Society for Human Rights (a secular group with members in thirty-eight states worldwide), 80% of all acts of religious discrimination in the world today are directed at Christians.

Was Christianity just a crutch for the 500 Christians hacked to death by machete-wielding Hindu radicals in Orissa, India? Was it just a comfort blanket for the thousands killed or displaced by the violence directed towards them in Syria and Iraq? Such arguments must sound rather strange to the 100,000 Christians who die every year because of their faith.

Many come to believe in Jesus not because they wanted it to be true, but actually despite the fact that they didn't want it to be true! One of the original leaders of the Christian church, the apostle Paul, started out as a persecutor of the Christian faith. He didn't desire Christianity to be true – he wanted to destroy it. C. S. Lewis spent much of his life as an atheist. When as an adult he came to believe in God, he described himself as being perhaps 'the most dejected and reluctant convert in all England'.[23] And there are many others who have come to Christian faith not because they wanted it to be true, but in spite of the fact that they didn't.

There exists today, however, a form of Christianity that *could* be seen as wish-fulfilment, but it is not the genuine Christianity of the Bible. It's a representation of Christianity, often seen on television, where you are promised that you can have whatever you like. The televangelist claims any material blessing can all be yours as long as you follow Jesus (and, incidentally, give lots of money to the preacher). Such a view is a million miles from the Christianity of the Bible. Jesus never promised that following him would be easy, or that we would get everything we want. His call was to take up a cross, deny oneself and follow him.[24]

The evidence does not support the idea that Christianity is just a wish-fulfilment. Nor does it support the idea that people's beliefs are determined only by our social upbringing. If this were the case, then how could anyone ever change their beliefs? For not everyone stays in the religion of their parents. It isn't just atheists who may have different beliefs from their parents – it would also be true of the entire first generation of Christians!

There are many people around the world who have come to faith in Jesus from different cultural and religious backgrounds. Some made the decision at great personal cost, like one of my friends, who will remain nameless. When he told his family that he had become a Christian, they threatened to kill him, so he had to flee the country for his own safety. The idea that our beliefs are just determined by our culture would sound very strange to Christians in Algeria, Iran and Mongolia – three of the countries where the Christian church is growing most rapidly today. And almost none of these believers comes from a Christian family.

The biggest problem

We have seen that neither the argument from the angle of psychology nor the argument from sociology explains away belief in God. The biggest issue is that while they might explain *why* people believe what they do, they won't actually help us discover whether God does indeed exist. *If* God doesn't exist, then psychology and sociology can provide very good arguments for why many people will still believe. However, if there is actually a God, then the very same arguments, turned around, provide an equally good explanation for why people don't believe in him.

To discover what is actually true, we would need to move beyond the objections from psychology and sociology and look at the evidence. So it's to the evidence that we now turn.

Further reading

) Amy Orr-Ewing, *But Is It Real? Answering 10 Common Objections to the Christian Faith* (IVP, 2008)

〉〉 Armand M. Nicholi, Jr, *The Question of God: C. S. Lewis and Sigmund Freud Debate God, Love, Sex, and the Meaning of Life* (Simon & Schuster, 2003)

〉〉 Andrew Sims, *Is Faith Delusion? Why Religion Is Good for Your Health* (Continuum, 2011)

〉〉〉 Keith Ward, *More Than Matter? What Humans Really Are* (Lion Books, 2010)

4. BUT DON'T YOU NEED EVIDENCE?

'There's not one shred of evidence that God exists!' exclaimed one student after my talk. He continued, 'You will never be able to prove that there is a God.'

Another said, 'I know I can't prove that God *doesn't* exist, but then I also can't *prove* that there aren't fairies at the bottom of the garden, but that doesn't mean I should believe it!'

We have seen that psychology and sociology can help us understand *why* people believe what they believe, but they don't actually help us discover whether what they believe is true. For that, we need to turn to the evidence. Yet many people would point out that this is exactly where the problem lies . . .

Richard Dawkins put it this way at the conclusion of a letter to his daughter, published in his book *A Devil's Chaplain*:

Next time that somebody tells you something is true, why not say to them: 'What kind of evidence is there for that?' And if

they can't give you a good answer, I hope you'll think very
carefully before you believe a word they say.
Your loving Daddy[1]

So, what is the evidence?

We will look at four different pieces. The first three could
be classed as 'clues' that point us towards God. The fourth,
you might say, is more con'*clu*'sive! It is important to remember that we are not looking for proofs: there are very few
things that we can prove 100%. However, we will be asking:
what is the most reasonable explanation for the evidence that
we have?

The universe exists

If you had asked Bertrand Russell, a famous atheist of a
previous generation, 'Why does the universe exist?', he would
have told you that it always had done. He stated, 'The idea
that things must have had a beginning is really due to the
poverty of our imagination.'[2] Until the middle of the twentieth
century many would have believed in an infinite universe.
There was no need for a creator, for the universe had always
existed. However, this is no longer the case today.

The idea of an infinite past was never without difficulty.
For a start, the concept of infinity in reality, rather than just
in theory, is a notoriously difficult one.[3]

The scientific evidence against such a view became apparent
during the last century, particularly through the work of a
Belgian cosmologist, Georges Lemaître (interestingly, also
a Catholic priest). It became increasingly apparent that the
universe was not static, but expanding. From this, we could
extrapolate back and find that the universe would have had to
have been smaller and smaller until eventually it would have

been a single point. Therefore, it seemed that the universe had a beginning. Yet it also became clear that it was not just the universe that began; so too did space and time. This beginning became known as 'the Big Bang'.

I have often been asked how, as a Christian, I could square my belief in the Bible with the evidence for the Big Bang. This really isn't the hurdle people think it is. In a number of ways, it fits completely with what Christian theology has always held to. The Bible affirms that space, time and matter had a beginning. Many would argue that science has only just discovered what the Bible has said all along! At the very least, we can say that the evidence for the beginning of the universe seems to fit much more naturally within a theistic worldview than an atheistic one. This is evidenced by the fact that initially it was atheists who had a bigger problem with the idea of the Big Bang. In fact, the term itself was originally intended to mock the idea!

If the universe had a beginning, then it naturally leads to the question of what caused it to begin. Sir Arthur Eddington, Lemaître's tutor at Cambridge, admitted that the idea 'was repugnant to him', and that he 'would like to find a genuine loophole'.[4] Much more recently, Stephen Hawking has said, 'People do not like the idea that time has a beginning, probably because it smacks of divine intervention.'[5]

There is a fascinating irony in all of this. We are often fearful that belief in God could hinder the progress of science, because people would be driven more by their philosophy and less by the evidence. Yet, in this case, exactly the same could be said for the atheistic worldview. The difficulty that so many had with the theory of the Big Bang was not the insufficient evidence, but rather the philosophical implications – it seemed to increase the plausibility of God's existence.

So, how have people tried to avoid letting God get a 'divine foot in the door'? How might we explain the beginning of the universe if there is no God?

Option one: The law of gravity
In his book *A Brief History of Time*, Stephen Hawking alluded to being open to the question of God. However, he then caused a media sensation in 2010 with the publication of *The Grand Design*. In it he publicly rejected the need for God in regard to the beginning of the universe. *The Times* ran the headline: 'Hawking: God did not create the universe'. In the book he explained, 'It is not necessary to invoke God to light the blue touch paper to set the universe going . . . Because there is a law of gravity, the universe can and will create itself out of nothing.'[6]

Despite writing sixty-three years before Hawking, C. S. Lewis has a very good response: 'To think the laws can produce it is like thinking that you can create real money by simply doing sums. For every law, in the last resort, says "if you have A, then you will get B", but first catch your A: the laws won't do it for you.'[7] Laws do not create. They only explain.

The story is told of some scientists who figure out how to create life. They go to God and say, 'OK, God, we've finally figured out how you did it; we could do it all without you now in the lab, so thanks for everything, but we won't be consulting you any more.' 'Wow,' God replies, 'that's amazing, how did you do it?' The scientists show him their laboratory. 'We just passed this electric current through this pile of dust.' 'So that's how it works,' God says, 'but you'll be needing to find your own dust.'

Hawking may have changed his mind on the possibility of God's existence, but he hasn't shown any new reasons as to why God should not exist. So, why should we believe his conclusion any more now than before?

Option two: A universe from nothing

In his book of the same title, Lawrence Krauss has also sought to explain how there could be *a universe from nothing*. He stated, 'Nothing is a physical concept, because something is a physical concept. What we've learned is that the nothing of "empty space" is actually a lot more complicated than you might have imagined . . .'[8]

If that sounds rather confusing to you, then you're not alone! When Krauss refers to 'nothing', he means a lot more than nothing. It *is* something![9] It reminds me of what happens when you discover a child up to some kind of mischief, and you ask them what they are doing. 'Nothing,' comes back the guilty reply, which invariably means quite the opposite! *A Universe from Something*, while being a far more accurate title, would not be quite so attention grabbing! It would also still very much beg the question: 'Where did the something come from?'

Reviewing the book in the *New York Times*, quantum physicist David Albert concludes, 'Krauss is dead wrong and his religious and philosophical critics are absolutely right.'[10] He explains, 'The fact that particles can pop in and out of existence, over time, as those fields rearrange themselves, is not a whit more mysterious than the fact that fists can pop in and out of existence, over time, as my fingers rearrange themselves. And none of these poppings – if you look at them aright – amounts to anything even remotely in the neighborhood of a creation from nothing.'[11]

Option three: An oscillating universe

Others have suggested that the universe is continually expanding and contracting. In this way, the Big Bang was not the start of space-time and matter, but simply the latest phase in an infinite past of oscillations. Yet it has been pointed out that this would go against the second law of thermodynamics (the idea that things move from a state of order to chaos – a good example of this being a typical student bedroom over the duration of the academic year!). Things cannot go on expanding and contracting forever. So this still leaves the question of how, when and where everything came from in the first place.

So, what is the best explanation for the beginning of the universe? The ultimate question is: 'Why is there anything and not nothing?'

While the discovery of the beginning of the universe posed a problem for the atheist, it didn't really pose the same difficulty for the theist. In fact, it fitted with what many had always thought. According to the biblical worldview, God is outside space and time, and responsible for its creation.

Some will immediately ask, as one student in Serbia did recently, 'If God created the universe, then who created God?' But the problem is that the question doesn't make sense. The God of the Bible, by definition, is eternal and uncreated. Therefore, the question could be rephrased: 'Who created the uncreated being?' It would not make logical sense. God is not a physical contingent being, needing a cause. He is the unmoved mover, the uncaused cause. Even if you don't believe in that God, it's important to know what we're talking about and to recognize that the question 'Who created God?' doesn't make sense.

Does this absolutely prove that God exists? No, but we must decide which explanation makes best sense of the evidence that a universe exists at all.

This universe exists

The next piece of evidence follows hot on the heels of the Big Bang. In fact, I would say, very hot indeed, for it regards what happened in the first fraction of a second after the Big Bang. The conditions at the beginning had to be just right for our universe to have had the capability of giving rise to life. Not only this, but the constants of the laws of physics needed to be accurate to a very, very high degree for life to be possible; constants such as the force of gravity or the electromagnetic force responsible for holding atoms together all required enormous precision.[12] Physicist Paul Davies explains, 'Like the porridge in the tale of Goldilocks and the three bears, the universe seems to be "just right" for life, in so many intriguing ways.'[13]

One of these examples, put forward by the Oxford cosmologist Sir Roger Penrose, concerns the initial entropy of the universe. He explains that there was a 1 in $10^{10^{123}}$ chance of this universe existing. To give you an idea of how big that number is, he explains that if you wanted to write it out in full by writing a nought on every atom in the universe, this would be impossible, since there are only 10^{80} atoms in the known universe![14]

The incredible fine-tuning of the universe for life compels us to ask whether it was designed to be this way.

The incredible fine-tuning of the universe for life compels us to ask whether it was designed to be this way. 'It seems as though someone has fine-tuned nature's numbers to make the universe . . . The impression of design is overwhelming,'[15] says Paul Davies. Fred Hoyle appears to agree: 'A common sense interpretation of the facts suggests that a super-intellect has monkeyed with the laws of physics, chemistry and biology, and that there are no blind forces worth speaking about in nature.'[16] This is all the more significant given that earlier in his life he had described religion as an illusion.

Using Bayes Theorem (a theory for calculating probability), John Hawthorne, Professor of Philosophy at Oxford University, shows that even if we previously held that there was a very minimal possibility of the existence of God, the discovery of such fine-tuning must dramatically increase the probability that he exists.[17]

The incredible fine-tuning of the universe certainly seems to point in the direction of it having been designed that way. How could we explain it if we didn't believe in God?

Option one: It just happened?

Some will point out that although the chances of the universe being fine-tuned for life are small, the fact that we are here at all just goes to show that it happened, for if it hadn't, then we wouldn't be here to read about it!

However, is it really that simple? Imagine you are standing before a line of fifty highly trained sharp shooters waiting to be executed (not a very pleasant thought, I grant you). From a short distance they all fire, and yet you find that every single one of them has missed. Now, you could explain your survival as luck: after all, if they hadn't missed, you wouldn't be alive to think about it. However, it is much more likely that you would ask the question: was there some reason why they all missed? It would be hard to accept that it was just an accident.[18]

Or imagine that I win a lottery. Now, the chances of me doing so are low, but you could argue that someone will probably win (especially if many play) . . . but then, imagine if I won the lottery again next week, and the week after, and every week for the next year. Do you think that the owners of the lottery would just shrug their shoulders and put it down to luck? Or would they start an investigation to find out if the lottery-number-picking machine had been rigged?

Option two: A multiverse?

One idea that seeks to explain the apparent fine-tuning of our universe is that of a multiverse, a whole plethora of billions upon billions (some would even suggest an infinite number) of universes. This has gained significant popularity with many atheists due to their belief that it might avoid the involvement of a creator. Among such a large number of different universes, some would say that it is not surprising that one would be fine-tuned for life. And we happen to live in one of the ones that was. Theoretical physicist Andrei Linde explains that if there were only one universe, then 'we'd need to speculate about the divine cause' that made life possible, whereas if there are many universes 'the world we live in makes perfect sense'.[19]

To use a lottery illustration again, if only one person enters, then the chances of their being a winner are very, very small indeed. However, if several million people buy tickets (as they do), then it is much more probable that one of them will be the winner. In the same way, we could say that we 'happen to live in the universe that holds the winning ticket'.

However, there are multiple difficulties that we encounter with the idea of a multiverse.[20] For instance, it doesn't necessarily get rid of the issue of fine-tuning, but just takes it back a step further – to the fine-tuning not simply of this universe, but the fine-tuning that enabled there to be a multiverse in the first place.

Perhaps an even more significant issue is that in postulating the idea of a multiverse, we have actually moved beyond the realm of science. John Polkinghorne, the theoretical physicist, explains, 'Let us recognise these speculations for what they are. They are not physics, but, in the strictest sense, metaphysics.'[21]

We must ask whether the idea of a multiverse really springs from the evidence. Rather, is it not more often an attempt to avoid the implication that God might indeed be responsible for the fine-tuning of our universe? Polkinghorne continues, 'A possible explanation of equal intellectual respectability – and to my mind greater economy and elegance – would be that this one world is the way it is, because it is the creation of the will of a Creator who purposes that it should be so.'[22]

Back to 'God of the gaps'?

When I made these points recently in a debate, my 'opponent' responded by asking, 'Aren't you just going back to a "God of the gaps", accrediting God with the things that we don't understand?'

The accusation is unfair, for the questions that we have looked at don't arise from our ignorance of science, but from our increased knowledge of it! These are questions that go beyond the observable universe and the realm of science. You could even turn the accusation around, and ask whether some are not guilty of coming up with a 'science of the gaps'. There is a danger that we might naively assume that science will eventually have the answer to every question, even when the question has gone beyond its scope.

Values exist

Christmas is always a complicated and expensive time for my extended family. Having five siblings and an ever-increasing number of nieces and nephews, buying presents can be a challenge. Once I bought my nephew one very big Lego set (partly because I wanted to play with it too!) and bought his sister several smaller presents. Ultimately, though, I had spent the same amount of money on each child. Unaware of this, my nephew exclaimed, 'It's not fair! She's got five presents, and I've only got one!' How interesting that, even as a child, there was already an acute awareness of injustice (even though not altogether accurate). Where did that sense of justice come from?

This is a serious issue, because the question of justice goes far deeper than the number of Christmas presents we receive. We live in a world of horrific violence and evil. Just this morning I read in a newspaper of a group of women having been burnt alive for their refusal to take part in violent sex acts with their terrorist captors. In another city nearby, children have been systematically decapitated by the invading forces.

Yet the world is not totally evil or without goodness. Less publicized, but no less real, are the thousands of selfless acts of love and mercy that take place each day: medics risking their lives treating victims of contagious diseases; volunteers flying into earthquake zones to hunt for survivors, despite the risk of serious aftershocks; the unsung heroes daily continuing to care for the disabled, the sick and the vulnerable.

How do we distinguish between what is good and evil? We all make value judgments every day, but where do these values come from? Could they not have something to do with God's existence? Scottish philosopher David Hume pointed out that you cannot get an 'ought' from an 'is'.[23] In other words, if all that exists is matter, then there is no logical way to determine objective moral values.

I have sometimes illustrated this[24] by showing an audience a picture of the famous Alexandros statue 'Venus de Milo'[25] and asking them what they see. Most people (with the exception of teenage boys who tend to notice something else) would reply, 'I see a woman without any arms', to which I ask, 'Why do you see that? What if I said to you that I just see a lump of rock?' The reason why people see a woman *without* arms is that they have a concept of what a woman *ought* to look like. We have an objective idea by which we can judge

the statue, but what is the objective basis whereby we can determine what *ought* to be and what *ought not* to be? C. S. Lewis explained this helpfully when he said, 'A man does not call a line crooked unless he has some idea of a straight line.'[26]

What is this plumb line by which we can make these judgments?

It would seem that the presence of an objective moral law would require the existence of an objective moral lawgiver. The existence of non-material things, such as values, seems to point to the fact that there must be more than just a materialistic universe.

This doesn't mean that making moral judgments depends on believing in God. The Bible indicates that God has given us all an inbuilt sense of what is right and wrong, whether we believe in him or not. The question is not: 'Can an atheist make moral judgments?' Rather: 'What is their foundation, and where do they come from, if not from God?'

Imagine if I didn't believe in the existence of power stations. I just assumed that electricity was self-generating and came out of the wall. Would my wrong belief mean that my phone won't charge when I plug it in? Of course not, but if there were no power stations, then I'd be stuck!

How might we explain values if there is no God?

Option one: Objective moral values don't exist

This is perhaps the most logically consistent conclusion. After a talk on the topic of 'suffering' at one university, I received this text during the question time: 'You argue that a broken world does not contradict God, but I would argue that a broken world assumes God, and you are creating your own paradoxes. The world is not broken; it is what it is.'

However, while such a view can seem fine theoretically in the detachment of a lecture room, it is quite another thing to live it out consistently. Can you really look at some of the horrific happenings around the world and say that they are not objectively evil?

A group of people who attempted to do this were the French existentialists. They sought to live consistently with the belief that there is ultimately no basis for morality or meaning. One of their leading thinkers was Albert Camus. Yet even he struggled to live out his own philosophy. His final novel *The Fall* seems to be a fascinating admission of his own sense of guilt that no matter how hard he tried, he could not explain it away.[27] We can dismiss the idea of objective right and wrong, but it's not always so easy to get rid of our own sense of guilt.

This was true for the German author and Nobel Prize winner Günter Grass. He had spent much of his life exposing those who had been part of the Nazis' dreaded SS, ruining the lives of many in the process. However, in his biography at the end of his life he admitted to having been part of it himself. When asked why he revealed this information, he said, 'It was weighing on my mind . . . It had to come out finally. It will stain me forever.'[28]

Option two: Culture defines what is right and wrong

Some suggest that our morality is a result of the society in which we live. We decide what is right and wrong, depending on the consensus of those around us. This is also why some societies have different standards of morality from those of others.

However, if this is the case, then what we regard as 'wrong' might actually be 'right' if we lived in a different society. I was speaking once in a philosophy class, and one of the students stated, 'If the Nazis had won the war, then we would all think that anti-Semitism is OK.' I asked her, 'So if the Nazis had won the war, would the Holocaust have been OK then?' Without any hesitation, she agreed. The rest of the room looked shocked. Most of them were of the view that even if the Nazis had won the war, and had successfully brainwashed us, the Holocaust would still have been an atrocious evil.

It's also worth asking the question: 'If morality is decided by the majority, then how do we ever change abuses in society?' Just over 200 years ago the majority of people in my country thought that slavery was acceptable. How would this ever have changed? It required the belief in a higher basis for morality to change the convictions of an entire society.

Option three: Morality evolved

If evolution is responsible for our biology, then could it not also be responsible for our morality? Can't we observe that morality has evolved, because to be moral is more beneficial for our survival? Isn't it possible to see a less-evolved form of morality practised in the animal kingdom? Even ants work together in a remarkably cooperative way.

However, it is more difficult than we might imagine to interpret morality by looking at the animal kingdom. Some animals help each other, while others eat each other. How do we decide which practice we might rather follow?

Another problem is that in a society of altruists, it will always be more beneficial to be selfish. So natural selection should always be pushing for the selection of selfishness over altruism. What is often called altruism in evolutionary biology is actually a form of selfishness.

It is also interesting that not everything that we would hold to as 'good or virtuous' is necessarily beneficial for survival and the passing on of our DNA. Some things would appear to be the opposite – such as the practice of self-sacrifice, caring for the severely disabled or remaining faithful to a spouse who is infertile. How should we explain such things? Richard Dawkins describes these as 'misfirings of evolution' and 'Darwinian mistakes', but is that all they are? Are some of the most commendable and beautiful actions simply mistakes? Dawkins does admittedly describe them as 'blessed precious mistakes', though it is not clear where he smuggles this value judgment from. Surely that too is simply the product of evolution and could equally be a mistake?

Option four: Moral values can be determined scientifically

In his book *The Moral Landscape*, Sam Harris, one of the leading New Atheists, claims that science alone can determine objective moral values. He suggests that we can scientifically assess which actions cause the least amount of suffering for the greatest number of people. In this way, we can then determine what actions are right and wrong.

The difficulty, though, lies right at the foundation of his argument. He explains, 'We simply must start somewhere. I am arguing that, in the moral sphere, it is safe to begin with the premise that it is good to avoid behaving in such a way as to avoid the worst possible misery for everyone.'[29]

However, on what basis does he determine that this is the case? He is smuggling in an assumption for which he has provided no explanation. It is not enough to say, 'We know this intuitively', for that would simply beg the question: 'Why do we know it intuitively?' The premise is itself a form of moral value. He has not explained what is moral by science. Rather, he has assumed what is moral (without explaining why), and then provided a quasi-scientific explanation for how to apply it in different situations.[30]

We have addressed three clues as to the existence of God: the fact that there is a universe at all, the initial fine-tuning of the universe and the existence of moral values. None of them proves the existence of God, but in comparison with the alternatives, we must ask which one provides the best explanation of the evidence? Does the evidence make more sense in a worldview with or without God in it? It certainly seems as if the clues are pointing in one direction.

However, are these 'clues' all we have to go on? Don't we have anything more con'*clu*'sive? (Sorry!) After all, the above arguments may point to the possibility of some kind of spiritual force, but they fall a long way short of revealing the God of the Bible.

God breaks in

If God does exist, then how could we ever know more about him? If he is the Creator and we are his creatures, then there is no reason, in theory, why we should ever know about him.

It would be like Harry Potter trying to discover J. K. Rowling! Yet what if J. K. Rowling brought out an eighth book in the series? But this time she writes herself into the story as the new principal of Hogwarts? Then it would be different!

The amazing, and unique, claim of Christianity is that God *has* written himself into the story of our world. He hasn't just provided clues to his existence, but he has stepped in, in person. The claim is that in Jesus of Nazareth, God has made himself clear, so that then we don't have to keep guessing.

Such a huge claim, of course, raises some serious questions. Wasn't Jesus just another myth, like so many others? How can we believe the miracle stories; aren't they impossible? How do we know that the accounts of Jesus' life weren't just made up? Haven't the details been distorted over the years? Did Jesus really even claim to be God? And could the resurrection from death really have happened?

These are important questions, so I have devoted the second half of this book to examining them in detail. If Jesus is the greatest evidence for God, then a careful examination of the evidence for him is important. Yet, ironically, it seems this is what so many atheists have failed to do.[31]

Further reading

❭ John C. Lennox, *God and Stephen Hawking: Whose Design Is It Anyway?* (Lion Books, 2011)

❭ C. S. Lewis, *Mere Christianity* (HarperCollins, 1952)

❭ Keith Ward, *Why There Almost Certainly Is a God: Doubting Dawkins* (Lion Books, 2008)

❭❭ Rodney Holder, *Big Bang, Big God: A Universe Designed for Life?* (Lion Books, 2013)

❭❭ William Lane Craig, *Reasonable Faith: Christian Truth and Apologetics* (Crossway, 2008)

)) John Polkinghorne, *Quarks, Chaos and Christianity: Questions to Science and Religion* (Crossroad, 2006)

))) William A. Dembski and Michael Ruse, *Debating Design: From Darwin to DNA* (Cambridge University Press, 2007)

))) Antony Flew, *There Is a God: How the World's Most Notorious Atheist Changed His Mind* (HarperOne, 2008)

))) William Lane Craig and J. P. Moreland (eds.), *The Blackwell Companion to Natural Theology* (Wiley-Blackwell, 2012)

))) Richard Swinburne, *The Existence of God* (Clarendon Press, 2004)

5. BUT ISN'T JESUS JUST ANOTHER MYTH?

A teacher called one of the children up after class.

'Jonny, I think you've been copying in your exam,' he explained.

'No, Sir! Not me, Sir!' Jonny replied.

'I think you have,' repeated the teacher. 'I have your paper here, and also the paper of Tommy who sat next to you. For the first question, Tommy has written that the answer is 2, and you have written that the answer is 2 – and you are both right!'

'So what, Sir?' Jonny appealed.

'Well,' the teacher continued, 'for the second question, Tommy has written that the answer is 10, and you have written that the answer is 10, and you are both wrong!'

'It still doesn't prove anything!' Jonny retorted.

'There's more,' said the teacher. 'For the third question, Tommy has written "I don't know", and you have written "I don't know either"!'

Copying in exams is nothing new . . . but a more serious claim often made against Christianity is that the early Christians engaged in their own plagiarism.

'Jesus is no evidence for God! Most of the stories of Jesus were simply copied from other myths that existed long before his time. Horus, Dionysus and Mithra are basically the same as Jesus!'

This was one of the responses of my 'opponent' in a recent debate on the existence of God. In his view, no further investigation into Jesus was necessary, for the story was a myth, and not even an original myth at that.

While this is certainly not a new idea, it has become more popular in recent years. In Dan Brown's *The Da Vinci Code*, one of the characters (Leigh Teabing) asserts,

> Nothing in Christianity is original. The pre-Christian God Mithras – called the *Son of God* and the *Light of the World* – was born on December 25, died, was buried in a rock tomb, and then resurrected in three days. By the way, December 25 is also the birthday of Osiris, Adonis, and Dionysus. The new-born Krishna was presented with gold, frankincense, and myrrh. Even Christianity's weekly holy day was stolen from the pagans.[1]

The same idea comes up in the films *Zeitgeist* and *Religulous*,[2] and the popular TV comedy quiz show *QI*.[3] If I had a pound for every time the argument has been made in a discussion, I would be a rich man!

So, were the early Christians guilty of copying? Is Christianity just a forgery of earlier ideas? Should we reject Jesus as any sort of evidence for God?

Well, it will hardly surprise you to find that I don't think so.

Christianity isn't just another myth

The evidence *against* Christianity being just another myth is so overwhelming that it hardly seems fair to discuss it. People may imagine that I am picking on a straw man. However, it is important to discuss this, for, as with so many factoids, it has been repeated enough times to give the impression that it might be true. It's also worth looking at because the idea of Christianity being a myth might actually have more in it than even the authors of these arguments realize.

The belief that Jesus was just a reinvention of pagan myths became popular at the end of the nineteenth century. One of the key proponents was a poet called Gerald Massey,[4] who fancied himself as an Egyptologist, though it seems his poetry was a lot better than his Egyptology! Although his ideas attracted some interest at the time, scholars soon rejected them as fanciful. It would be very difficult, if not impossible, to find support for his work from any genuine Egyptologist today.

So what are we to make of the supposed parallels?

Similarities do not prove a link

I wonder if you have heard of the Morgan Robertson novel *Futility, or the Wreck of the Titan?* It was about the sinking of a supposedly unsinkable ocean liner, *The Titan*, after she hit an iceberg in the North Atlantic. Many lives were lost because necessary lifeboats had been removed before the sailing. Not very original, you may think. Except that this novel was published in 1898, fourteen years before the sinking of the actual *Titanic*.

The parallels are fascinating. Yet no-one doubts that, just because of the existence of an earlier fictitious story, there really was a ship called *Titanic* which sank. Though the parallels are extraordinary, there is no evidence that the stories were connected at all.

Similarly, you will probably immediately recognize the details of the following terrible event. A plane took off from an airport in Massachusetts and crashed into a skyscraper in New York City. It collided with the building between the seventy-eighth and eightieth floors, leading to the deaths of everyone on board, as well as many people in the building. Almost all of us would identify this as being one of the planes involved in the horrific attacks of 9/11. However, all these details are also true of another event fifty-six years earlier, when a B25 bomber crashed into the Empire State Building. The fact that both events are so similar doesn't mean that we disbelieve the later events, or suggest that the 9/11 bombers got their ideas from the incident in 1945.

Sometimes history throws up surprising similarities, but this does not prove that these events are linked, or caused by each other. In the same way, similarities in the stories of Jesus and some pagan myths do not prove that the stories are linked, or that the authors of the Gospels simply copied the early stories.

Are the parallels between Jesus and myths actually there?

The examples we have just seen are far more fascinating than the parallels that actually exist between the pagan myths and Jesus. When we start to unpack the evidence, it appears that the supposed parallels are either vastly exaggerated or simply not there.

- *Some of the parallels are made up.* There's no evidence that the Egyptian god Horus was thought to have been born of a virgin, was visited by wise men at his birth, had twelve followers, walked on water, was crucified or was resurrected.[5] There is also no evidence that any of this is supposed to have happened to Mithra.[6] Stories of Mithra don't claim he was born of a virgin, but that he appeared out of a rock. There was no suggestion of resurrection, for it is believed that he never even died. The events attributed to Osiris after his death were not a resurrection, but could be more accurately described as zombification.[7] Again and again, the supposed parallels fail to materialize when you actually examine the evidence.

- *Some of the parallels are confused.* It is rather fascinating that much is made of the idea that Horus, Mithra and co. were all born on December 25. Aside from the fact that there is often no evidence for this, one wonders why the point is even being made: no Christian I know actually claims that December 25 was the actual birthday of Jesus. That date was picked more than a century later to commemorate the event. Furthermore, my friends in Eastern Europe would be even more bemused by this supposed parallel, given that they celebrate Christmas on 7 January.[8]

- *Some of the parallels are hardly surprising.* For instance, you would expect people to claim that their gods performed miracles – you might even say it comes with the job description. Similarly, it is hardly surprising that they were adored at their birth – most babies are. The idea that they had followers, or that they taught others, is not exactly ground-breaking.

- *Most of the parallels are the wrong way round.* If the claim is that Christians borrowed ideas from the older myths, one would assume that those ideas must already have been around in the first century. Yet most of the sources referred to actually come later. If any copying was being done, then you could even argue that it was the other way round.

What was the true context of Christianity?

People who suggest that Jesus is just a reinvention of pagan myths seem to neglect the detail that Christianity, in its origins, was a profoundly Jewish movement. Jesus was a Jew, and all of his first disciples were too. Surely, it would be more beneficial to see that the causal connections actually stem from this context. We could question, 'Is it more likely that the early Christians got the idea of twelve disciples from the twelve signs of the zodiac or from the twelve tribes of Israel?'

It's also rather incredible to think that the early Jewish Christians, who had real issues with whether they could even eat meat that had been sacrificed to pagan gods,[9] would choose to base their whole religion on the biographies of those same gods. It is significant that the idea of Jesus being a type of pagan myth arose when it did. James Crossley, Professor of Bible, Society and Politics at St Mary's University, Twickenham, explains,

> In the late-nineteenth and early-twentieth centuries, there was a major tendency to understand Jesus in terms of 'race'. A part of this tendency was to 'de-Judaize' Jesus and even claim that he was of Aryan descent. This was, unsurprisingly, a view taken up in Nazi scholarship which, at the time, was part of the mainstream.[10]

It is the Jewish, not the pagan, context which gives us the best understanding of the life of Jesus. We see him fulfil what God had called the nation of Israel to do – but they had so often failed.

Old Testament Israel	Jesus
Called God's Son[11]	Called the Son of God
Came out of Egypt after being in slavery	Came out of Egypt after being a refugee
Wandered in the wilderness for forty years	Was tempted in the wilderness for forty days
Passed through the River Jordan on the way into the Promised Land	Was baptized in the same River Jordan by John the Baptist

While there were many ancient parallels between Judaism and Jesus, there was one event that was totally unexpected – the resurrection. The Jews had a belief in a final resurrection at the end of time, but the idea of one man coming back from the dead in the middle of history was totally unheard of. No-one was expecting that. This causes us to ask the question: 'If the idea of Jesus' resurrection was so unexpected and without parallel, why then did people believe it?' (We will look at that in chapter 10.)

So, we have seen that the story of Jesus hasn't been plagiarized from earlier myths. However, the surprising thing is that, in some ways, we could also say that it *is* a myth! What exactly do I mean?

Christianity is a myth!

When we use the word 'myth', we often simply mean a story that is not true. However, that definition isn't itself strictly true! There is a lot more to a myth than that. Myths are stories that *could* be true, inasmuch as they provide an explanation for the world as we know it. They resonate with our experience of life. Think of *The Lord of the Rings*. Tolkien sought to write a myth that would explain something of the way the world is. He did this in part by writing stories that would account for the origins of our language. For instance, the word 'Mordor' is the Old English word for 'murder'. 'Sauron' comes from Old Norse and means 'abominable'. The myths retell a familiar theme where heroism and rescue come from an unlikely source, where good defeats evil and hope is rekindled.

Among Tolkien's good friends in Oxford was C. S. Lewis. While Tolkien was a Christian, Lewis was an atheist. Lewis's big objection to Christianity was that it was just another myth. He was an expert in myths and legends, and while he loved them, he knew that they weren't true. One night the two were walking after dinner by the River Cherwell. Lewis expressed again his doubts about Christianity. Tolkien's response was surprising. He declared that Christianity was indeed a myth! Unlike the other myths, though, this was the myth that had actually happened. Every great myth was an echo of this one.

For Lewis, this was a defining moment. He later came to describe Christianity as 'the true myth'. He wrote,

> The heart of Christianity is a myth which is also a fact. The old myth of the dying God, without ceasing to be myth, comes down from the heaven of legend and imagination to the earth of history. It happens – at a particular date, in a particular place, followed by definable historical consequences. We pass from a Balder or an Osiris, dying nobody knows when or where, to a historical person crucified (it is all in order) under Pontius Pilate. By becoming fact, it does not cease to be myth: that is the miracle.[12]

This is the ultimate difference between Jesus and Horus, Mithra or any of the pantheon of gods. The story of Jesus actually took place, in real space and time. The authors of the accounts in the Gospels weren't making up fairy tales, but were recording what had actually happened. We can investigate their claims and look at the primary evidence (which we'll do in chapter 7). Funnily enough, looking at primary evidence is not something the proponents of the 'Jesus myth' idea seem very much inclined to do.

So, why is the idea still so popular?

Before we finish this chapter, it's worth asking one final question. If it is so clear that the early Christians didn't copy from pagan myths, why do so many people still claim that they did so? What makes the conspiracy stories so appealing?

It is not the evidence for the idea, but the implications of it that are so appealing. Such conspiracy theories feed on our distrust of authority – be it government or, in this case, the church (or in the case of *Zeitgeist*, the movie, both!). It certainly seems plausible (and, for many, convenient) to think that the church has been responsible for hiding the truth about Jesus. This idea builds on our suspicions about the established church and gives us another reason to reject Christianity.

The reality is that the 'conspiracy' is not what we might expect. The Jesus so often suppressed by the institution of the church is not the mythical, married, merely human Jesus of Dan Brown, but the very Jesus of the Bible. So dangerous is the real Jesus of history that 600 years ago, in England, it was illegal to own a copy of the Bible in your own language. The real Jesus of the Bible undermined abusive religious authorities and opposed hypocrisy. Often the established church feared that if people were to discover the real Jesus of the Bible, they would be able to see how far removed many of their teachings had become. Therefore, the best way to fight against the failures of the institutional church is not to get rid of Jesus as a myth, but to get back to the real Jesus of the Bible.

But can we really take the Jesus of the Bible seriously when the stories about him include so many miracles? Can anyone really believe in miracles today? That's the next subject we will investigate.

Further reading

❭ Paul Barnett, *Finding the Historical Christ* (Eerdmans, 2009)

❭ Tom Wright, *The Original Jesus: The Life and Vision of a Revolutionary* (Eerdmans, 1997)

❭❭ F. F. Bruce, *The New Testament Documents: Are They Reliable?* (Eerdmans, 2003)

❭❭ Charles Foster, *The Jesus Inquest: Myth or History?* (Monarch, 2006)

❭❭ James Patrick Holding (ed.), *Shattering the Christ Myth: Did Jesus Not Exist?* (Xulon Press, 2008)

❭❭❭ Richard Bauckham, *Jesus and the Eyewitnesses: The Gospels as Eyewitness Testimony* (Eerdmans, 2008)

❭❭❭ N. T. Wright, *The Resurrection of the Son of God* (Fortress Press, 2003)

6. BUT AREN'T MIRACLES IMPOSSIBLE?

It is rather strange that the majority of my compatriots say they don't believe in miracles, when, every four years, many of them are convinced we are going to win the World Cup! For my international friends, that would seem miraculous indeed! When we think about the miracles recorded in the Bible, we are obviously referring to something different from an unlikely event such as the miracle of English football success.

Nor are the miracles of the Bible just amazing yet naturally occurring events, such as the 'miracle' of childbirth. The miracles we are examining here are those occurrences that seem to happen outside the usual laws of nature. Could these kinds of miracles ever take place?

I had been leading a tour of the Middle East, taking in many of the significant locations in the life of Jesus. At each spot we had opened the Bible and read the accounts of what had happened. On the penultimate evening we were sitting by the shore of the Sea of Galilee, sipping drinks and watching the moon rise over the far horizon. In conversation with one of the guests, I reflected on the trip. I commented on how amazing it was to be in the very places where so many of the Bible events had taken place. She looked at me incredulously and exclaimed, 'You don't *actually believe* any of it, do you?' She continued, 'I'm a medical doctor; it would be impossible for me to believe in such ridiculous stories!'

To many people, the events in the Bible seem to fit into the same category as fairy tales: walking on water; a virgin getting pregnant; storms being stilled; sick being healed, and the dead coming back to life. It sounds as if these events should belong in the same world as Aladdin and his lamp, Peter Pan or Father Christmas. The Bible seems to be describing a very different world of events from the one we experience today.

Some try to get around this by 'cleansing' the Bible of the miraculous parts and just keeping to its general teaching. They say it is not necessary to believe all the stories in order to believe the main message. One person who literally did this was Thomas Jefferson. He physically cut and pasted sections of the New Testament in order to form the *Jefferson Bible* – a version devoid of any of the miracles of Jesus, but still retaining his ethical teaching.[1] The problem is that the miracles in the Bible are not 'extras on the edge of the plate' that you can take or leave at will (like broccoli and spinach). They form part of the central message: the main thing. In fact, Christianity without miracles would be like a roast dinner without the roast!

The early Christians were quick to assert that if you take the supernatural out of Christianity, you have nothing left. They claimed that the very foundation of the Christian faith was the most outlandish claim of all – the resurrection of Jesus Christ from the dead. One of the authors of the Bible put it this way: 'If Christ has not been raised, our preaching is useless and so is your faith.'[2]

Why do we find the idea of miracles so hard to believe? You might think it is simply a lack of evidence or experience of miracles that is to blame. However, could it be that our problem lies not initially with the evidence, but with our own assumptions? This was brought home to me during a conversation with a student in Warsaw, Poland. We had met several times, and he had voiced many objections to the Bible and the stories about Jesus. We spoke for over an hour about the reliability of the Bible and the evidence for the resurrection. After a while, when it appeared we were going round in circles, I asked him, 'If I could show you convincing evidence that the Bible was true, and that Jesus rose from the dead, would you believe?'

He shot back. 'You can't!'

'I didn't ask whether you think I can,' I replied, 'but rather that if I *could*, would you believe?'

'But you can't!' he repeated.

After repeating the question twice more and getting the same reply, I concluded, 'That's why this particular conversation has been a waste of time.'

'Why?' he asked, bemused.

'You've just told me that your problem is not a lack of evidence, rather that you've already assumed there could be no evidence. No matter what I say, you won't be convinced, because you have already determined that Jesus' resurrection must be impossible.'

Objections to the possibility of miracles happening take us back to our own assumptions about the universe. If my assumption is that there is no God, then of course miracles are impossible; we live in a closed system, and no such outside interference is possible. So when it comes to miracles, our first question has to do with our assumptions rather than the evidence. As C. S. Lewis said in his book on the subject, 'Those who want to assume that miracles cannot happen are merely wasting their time by looking into the texts: we know in advance what results they will find, for they have begun by begging the question.'[3]

But why are so many of us sceptical about claims of the miraculous? This has certainly not been the case throughout history, nor is it universally the case today.

Richard Dawkins gives us a clue when he says,

> The nineteenth century is the last time when it was possible for an educated person to admit to believing in miracles like the virgin birth without embarrassment. When pressed, many educated Christians are too loyal to deny the virgin birth and the resurrection. But it embarrasses them because their rational minds know that it is absurd, so they would much rather not be asked.[4]

But where did this embarrassment come from?

One factor was the rise of deism in the seventeenth century. This is the belief that God exists, but that he does not get involved in his creation. Clearly, in such a system, miracles would not be expected to occur. In the eighteenth century the philosopher David Hume, whom we met earlier, made a significant contribution to this discussion. My first introduction to him was while I was studying in his home town of Edinburgh – I used to cycle past his statue each week. Not everyone will have heard of Hume today, but his ideas will have had a big influence on our thinking on this topic. In particular, he presented the case for why he thought miracles were impossible:

> A miracle is a violation of the laws of nature; and as a firm and unalterable experience has established these laws, the

proof against a miracle, from the very nature of the fact, is as entire as any argument from experience as can be imagined . . . It is no miracle that a man, seemingly in good health, should die on a sudden: because such a kind of death, though more unusual than any other, has yet been frequently observed to happen. But it is a miracle that a dead man should come to life; because that has never been observed, in any age or country. There must, therefore, be a uniform experience against every miraculous event, otherwise the event would not merit that [description].[5]

From this and his other writing, we could summarize Hume's views as follows:

- Our experience of the world tells us that miracles do not happen. If miracles do happen, then they could no longer be described as such.
- The laws of nature do not allow for miracles to happen.
- Extraordinary claims require extraordinary evidence, but no such evidence exists.

Yet his arguments may not be as strong as they first appear.

Does our experience exclude miracles?

People's experience would seem to confirm that miracles do not take place. Indeed, very few people in the West today would claim that they have experienced or witnessed a miracle.

Miracles, by their very nature, are rare occurrences. If they happened all the time, then we wouldn't regard them as miracles. I remember speaking on the subject of the resurrection at a university mission. One student objected at the end and said, 'I can't believe that; things like that don't happen every day.'

'Exactly!' I replied. 'They don't! If they *did*, we wouldn't be talking about them, would we?'

It would appear, according to the Bible, that miracles most often occur at significant turning points in the history of God's relationship with humanity. Significantly, they cluster around three periods in the Bible: the giving of the Old Testament law (the story of Moses and the exodus), the ministry of the Old Testament prophets (notably Elijah and Elisha) and the start of the New Testament (Jesus and the beginning of the church). This seems to be quite deliberate, as we will see later. If miracles were not spread evenly throughout the time of the Bible, let alone throughout history more generally, then we shouldn't be surprised if we don't, personally, happen to see them today. In the same way, we shouldn't be surprised if, growing up in Africa, we didn't experience snow, or, if living in Norway, we had never experienced a drought. It's not that such things do not occur; it's just that we were not in the correct place and time to witness them personally.

So, personal experience of miracles is not essential. However, Hume's suggestion is total. He claims that *no-one* has ever experienced miracles. But we need to ask the question: 'How can we know that a miracle has never been experienced throughout history?' We cannot *absolutely* rule out the possibility; there is no way to investigate every event in the history of the universe! The only way we can know for sure that no miracles have ever taken place is if we already know that miracles are impossible, but in that case we would be starting by assuming what we are trying to prove. If we define a miracle as that which has never been experienced, then it is hardly surprising that we will never manage to find any evidence of it!

It would be a mistake to start by assuming that miracles cannot happen. It would be much wiser to say that, as far as we are aware, they have not happened, but that we remain open to the *possibility* that they might have done. A scientist might miss something of huge value if he rejected a new finding because it contradicted what he *thought* would happen, or what he thought was possible. By the same reasoning, we'd have to reject quantum mechanics, for its findings were a huge challenge to what was thought to be possible.

Lack of experience should not exclude miracles, but what about the laws of nature?

Do the laws of nature exclude miracles?

The second and seemingly stronger argument is that miracles would somehow be incompatible with science. Science describes for us the laws of nature, but were miracles to occur, then the laws of nature would have to go out of the window.

This argument is somewhat ironic, as we have already seen that the laws of nature themselves infer the existence of a lawgiver. Nancy Cartwright is one of the leading figures in the discussion of the laws of nature. She is suspicious of the way we too quickly say that science describes the laws of nature, precisely because it suggests God behind them. 'I think that in the concept of law there is a little too much of God,' she says, 'but in the end the concept of law does not make sense without the supposition of a lawgiver.'[6] The very idea of such universal laws is a result of monotheistic thinking.

So, would miracles break the laws of nature? Imagine that in my office drawer I have £200 in £10 notes. What would I do if I opened the drawer and discovered only £100? I wouldn't complain that the laws of arithmetic have been broken, rather that the laws of England have been broken – someone has nicked my cash![7]

Laws describe what normally happens, given no outside interference. If I drop my computer out of the window, it will, due to the law of gravity, no longer be a very effective computer. However, if someone caught the computer before it hit the ground, then it would not smash. The law of gravity would not have been broken; it just wouldn't have led to the expected outcome, as someone would have 'interfered'.

Could it not be that the One who created the very laws of nature could intervene in what he had made, at certain points, and introduce a new situation?

Could it not be that the One who created the very laws of nature could intervene in what he had made, at certain points, and introduce a new situation? This doesn't mean that the laws of nature no longer work, or have been broken, just that God's intervention has led to an unexpected outcome. Laws show us what *normally* happens. Far from making miracles impossible, it is the laws of nature that allow us to identify what a miracle is in the first place. Could there ever be enough evidence for such huge claims?

Is it possible that there is ever enough evidence for miracles?

If your friend came home from work and explained that earlier he had gone out for lunch with a colleague, you would probably have no reason to doubt what he claimed. If, though, he claimed that he had been temporarily abducted by an alien with whom he had shared a cheese sandwich, then you would probably be a little more sceptical! Extraordinary claims require extraordinary evidence for you to believe them.

In the same way, religions make some extraordinarily big claims. It would therefore be fair to expect that there should be good and convincing evidence if we are to believe them. In the case of Christianity, the good news is that there is.

Unlike many religious claims that are not objectively verifiable, the Christian faith opens itself up to such checking. The extraordinary claim about Jesus' divine identity is backed up by his resurrection from the dead – an event that is open to our investigation, and for which there is compelling evidence.

Hume claims that, to believe something, the alternative should be more 'miraculous' than the original claim. In other words, you should always believe the 'lesser miracle' – the one that is more likely. In one sense, I would agree that this is sensible. However, when it comes to the resurrection, the question is not simply: 'Is it more likely that Jesus stayed dead, or that he was raised?' (Then the answer would be simple.) We should rather ask, 'Given what we know of the events in question, what is the simplest explanation?' (We will address this issue in chapter 10.)

Another objection raised by Hume is that regularly occurring events are always more likely than events that are unique. So, if we were to base our convictions on what is most likely, then we would always have to rest with what commonly happens. This would discount the resurrection, for, normally, dead people stay dead, so it is more sensible to believe that Jesus did so too. However, it would be interesting to see where this logic of discounting singular events would lead you. Not only would you have to deny the resurrection, but you'd also have to reject the Big Bang. (In terms of singular events, they don't get much bigger than this!)

We have seen that despite our lack of experience, miracles don't have to be impossible, nor do they break the laws of nature. Rather, they represent God intervening to bring about an unexpected outcome. If sufficient evidence exists, then we should be able to believe that miracles are indeed possible. Therefore, rather than rejecting miracles on the basis of our previous assumptions, it would be much wiser actually to investigate the evidence for them, as we will do in the next chapter.

But before we do so, we will address one final uncertainty about miracles: 'What is the *point* of them? Aren't they rather arbitrary – unnecessary magic tricks? Why does God need to "show off" in such a way?'

What's the point of miracles?

Certainly, when I read of some miracles that are alleged to have happened, I am inclined to wonder what their purpose is. Some televangelists claim that God can turn your dental fillings to gold, and that he has miraculously provided them with a private jet! But do I really need golden fillings, and do they really need a private jet? In comparison to the needs of the world, these 'miracles' seem trivial and superficial. If God can make fillings golden, then, as one atheist website put it, 'Why won't God heal amputees?'[8]

However, the miracles of Jesus strike me as being categorically quite different from apparent miracles today. I think they have at least three purposes.

They are signs

Believing in the miracles of Jesus does not mean that we have to accept naively all claims of the miraculous, without any evidence. Some may claim that miracles happen today just as frequently as they did in the time of Jesus. While I don't discount the possibility of miracles today, I certainly don't think they are on the scale or frequency that we read about in the New Testament. If miracles happened all the time, then there would have been nothing unique or different about what Jesus did. If corpses often rose from the dead, then no-one would even bother talking about Jesus' resurrection. Even in the time-span during which the Bible was written (around 1,400 years), it seems that for large portions of that time no obvious miracles were taking place.

But what if, in the person of Jesus, God was doing something so significant that he wanted to draw everyone's attention to it? It is interesting that the New Testament never uses the word 'miracles', but rather defines them as 'signs'. They are designed to get our attention and to signify something of great importance.

They are gifts

If you or I had the same powers as Jesus, I wonder how we would use them? We could save a lot of money on ferry crossings, mass catering and beverages for a start! However, it is interesting that the miracles of Jesus were never for his own benefit, but always for the benefit of others. There are two occasions at the beginning and end of his ministry where Jesus is actively encouraged by others to use his powers for his own benefit. At the beginning of his public ministry, Jesus is in the desert and hasn't eaten for forty days. Just at that moment Satan turns up and tempts Jesus to use his powers to turn stones into bread and feed himself. Then, when dying on the cross, he is challenged by the crowd to save himself. He does neither. This is a God who wants to *give*, not to *get*. Jesus uses his power to care for others and not to serve himself.

This may leave us wondering why Jesus doesn't exercise his power to alleviate suffering today. If miracles can happen, then couldn't God do some more of them now?

This is a question I personally have asked for as long as I can recall. I remember as a young child hearing of the tragic and sudden death of one of my sister's friends. I lay awake at night, wondering why Jesus couldn't bring her back to life. After all, I had read stories in the Bible about how he had done this before.[9] I remember asking the question again, after a friend did appear to be dramatically healed. I was so glad of his recovery . . . but struggled to understand why it didn't happen to others.

It seems that Jesus can and sometimes does heal physically today, but in most situations he doesn't. While I have to admit that I don't fully have the answers to these questions, I am helped when I remember a third purpose of the miracles of Jesus.

They are snapshots of a wonderful future

Even in Jesus' own day there would have been many people who didn't get healed. We have a record of him raising three individuals back to life, but there would have been thousands of others who died during the same era, for whom he *didn't* do this.

However, in the miracles of Jesus we also have a snapshot of what the future will be like. Jesus began his public ministry by announcing that the kingdom of God was drawing near.[10] A new era was coming when God would transform the world and be King! What would this world be like? His miracles were a temporary demonstration of what would fully and finally happen one day. His kingdom would be a place where the sick are made well, the blind can see, the lame can walk, and the deaf can hear; a kingdom where funerals are cancelled and mourning is turned into celebration. It's a kingdom where the often-destructive fury of nature is brought under control. It's a kingdom that's characterized by a party with the best wine.

I don't know why God doesn't intervene when I see friends struggling with cancer, and remember others who have already died. It seems that God doesn't normally intervene now, but he has promised that one day he will do something even better. He will defeat death and end all suffering forever. In the meantime, he is able to give the grace and strength to keep going through tough situations.

A friend was recently diagnosed with a brain tumour. Despite the best medical care and the prayers of many, it remains unclear what his future will be. We long that he will be healed and live to see his newborn daughter grow up. Yet, despite the uncertainty of his future, he and his wife were able to write, 'We can't answer all the questions . . . but we know God has given us a way to know peace and hope in a sad situation . . . God promises that one day he will wipe away every tear from our eyes and will make everything new.'

Is this hope just an illusion? Or do we have reasons to think that Jesus really did do what the Bible claims he did?

Further reading

⟩ John Lennox, *Miracles: Is Belief in the Supernatural Irrational?* (Veritas Forum, 2013)

⟩⟩ Colin Humphreys, *The Miracles of Exodus: A Scientist's Discovery of the Extraordinary Natural Causes of the Biblical Stories* (HarperCollins, 2004)

⟩⟩ Craig S. Keener, *Miracles: The Credibility of the New Testament Accounts*, 2 vols. (Baker Academic, 2012)

⟩⟩ C. S. Lewis, *Miracles* (William Collins, 2002)

⟩⟩⟩ John Earman (ed.), *Hume's Abject Failure: The Argument against Miracles* (OUP USA, 2000)

⟩⟩⟩ R. Douglas Geivett and Gary R. Habermas (eds.), *In Defense of Miracles: A Comprehensive Case for God's Action in History* (IVP USA, 1997)

7. BUT AREN'T THE ACCOUNTS OF JESUS UNRELIABLE?

We saw in chapter 4 that the greatest evidence for God's existence is that he wrote himself into human history. Jesus was not just another mythical figure, but lived in real space and time. We also saw that we shouldn't reject those claims without first looking at the evidence. So, what is the evidence?

Even if we had only non-Christian sources, we could still discover a surprising amount about Jesus. For instance, we could discover that a man called Jesus existed, someone who was known for remarkable feats, and many people believed he was the Christ. He was crucified under the governorship of Pontius Pilate, but despite his ignominious death, the new movement of followers didn't die out. Instead, within a generation, the worship of Jesus spread as far as Rome. We can discover all these things without even opening a Bible.[1]

However, to find out significantly more about Jesus, we will need to turn to the primary sources. Four separate texts stand out as important. One early Christian writer referred to them as 'The memoirs of the apostles'.[2] More popularly, they are known as 'the Gospels' – Matthew, Mark, Luke and John – and they form the first four books of the New Testament. However, for many, this is exactly where the problem lies: 'If the main evidence for Jesus is to be found within the Bible, how can we trust it?'; 'They are "religious texts", so aren't they biased?'; 'Didn't the writers fabricate the stories?'; 'Weren't they made up much later, after the event?'

I remember chatting to a businessman on a bus in Serbia. Travelling across the Balkans on public transport can take quite a while, so we had plenty of time to chat. When the conversation turned to the topic of Jesus, his immediate response was: 'The stories about Jesus were made up hundreds of years later – you can't believe anything they say.'

Derren Brown, mentioned earlier, claims, 'The evidence shows very clearly that the stories of the New Testament were written in the first couple of hundred years after Jesus died. These stories then continued to be edited and revised for political and social needs for most of the first millennium.' He goes on to state that the early Christians 'needed stories and legends to inspire them and give them credence. So they created them . . .'[3]

A similar claim is made by Dan Brown (of confusingly similar name!). In his best-selling book *The Da Vinci Code*, he claims that the church deliberately suppressed the most reliable and early sources for Jesus' existence, and that these books present a very different picture of him. Of course, Dan Brown's work is fiction, but that doesn't stop it from casting serious doubt on the reliability of the Gospels. Richard Dawkins pointed out, 'The only difference between the gospels and *The Da Vinci Code* is that the gospels are ancient fiction while *The Da Vinci Code* is modern fiction.'[4] So, is there any hope of getting back to the real Jesus of history?

Two wrong assumptions

Before we examine the evidence, it is worth noting that there are two equal and opposite mistakes that people can make with the Bible. The first is to assume that the Bible *must* be true, just because it is the Bible. This mistake is often made by fundamentalist Christians – they don't even question whether the Bible is historically reliable. Such a view is obviously circular. The other mistake is to assume that the Bible *mustn't* be true, just because it is the Bible. This mistake is often made by atheists – they also don't even question whether the Bible is historically reliable!

I observed a clear instance of this latter mistake in an edition of *National Geographic* recently. The feature article was about Herod the Great, and began:

> [Herod] today is best known as the sly and murderous monarch
> of Matthew's Gospel, who slaughtered every male infant in
> Bethlehem in an unsuccessful attempt to kill the new-born
> Jesus . . . Herod is almost certainly innocent of this crime,
> of which there is no report apart from Matthew's account.[5]

However, why should we dismiss a claim just because it is found only in one source? The only time historians might do so is when other evidence suggests that it *cannot* be true. However, here the event in question certainly fits with what is known of Herod from other sources.[6] There is also no reason to think that other historians should record the event – Bethlehem was a small village, and this terrible event would have been overshadowed by some of Herod's other more high-profile atrocities. The author of the article clearly assumes that the Bible cannot be a reliable historical source. Please don't make the same mistake – you don't need to believe the Gospels are true before you start, but you do need to be open to the possibility that they might be.

It is also worth noting that whether or not the Bible is God's revealed word (as Christians have historically claimed) is not the issue here. We don't need to start by assuming that. The primary question is: 'Are the Gospels historically reliable?'

Can we treat the Gospels as real history?

Is there good reason to think that the Gospels record real history? Let's ask a number of questions of them, and see how they fare.

Who wrote them, and when?

The Gospels either claim to be written by eyewitnesses – as in the case of John – or, as with Luke, by those who had access to the eyewitness testimony. Luke begins his Gospel by explaining, 'since I myself have carefully investigated everything from the beginning, I too decided to write an orderly account for you'.[7]

It is intriguing that Luke records the names of some seemingly unimportant characters. For instance, in the story of two individuals who met Jesus after the resurrection, he names only one of them, Cleopas. It seems that this is the ancient equivalent to providing footnotes. In a society that valued oral testimony, Luke is giving his first readers the chance to go and check out the sources for themselves. In effect, he was saying, 'If you don't believe me, go ask them!'[8]

Many assume that the Gospels were made up long after the events they describe. This could not be the case. For a start, we have a fragment of John's Gospel (probably the last of the Gospels to be written) from between AD 125 and AD 150. We also know that, by the same time, the Gospels were obviously well enough known to be quoted or alluded to in the letters of Christian leaders, such as Clement, Ignatius and Polycarp.[9] It's quite hard to quote from a book that hasn't yet been written.

While we don't know exactly when in the first century the Gospels were written, the fact that they were not written later is important. It's much harder to make up a story when the eyewitnesses are still alive.

Weren't the supposed authors illiterate and uneducated?

Some point out that the Bible itself describes the apostles as 'unschooled, ordinary men',[10] so they question whether they could really have written the Gospels, or have been very reliable in what they wrote.

'Unschooled' didn't necessarily mean that these men were illiterate or stupid, but that they did not, like the Jewish leaders, have formal rabbinic training. In the same way, people can be wrongly dismissed today, simply because they didn't go to the 'right' university, or obtain certain letters after their name.

Why didn't the authors write them earlier?

It is commonly reckoned that there is a gap of approximately twenty to sixty years between Jesus' lifetime and the dates when the Gospels were written. So why didn't the authors produce them earlier? Wouldn't they have forgotten the details?

It is, of course, possible to forget details even in a shorter time-frame. I can't remember what I had for dinner last Wednesday . . . but I clearly remember what I ate when I went out for my first date (Pizza Hut, by the way – possibly the reason why it was the last one with that particular girl). You don't forget big events in life.

Psychologists have shown that certain events are far more memorable that others, for instance, those that are unique and unusual, and that affect us personally and emotionally.[11] The types of events described in the Gospels fit into these categories. They are not the kinds of things you would easily forget.

In the first century people relied on oral testimony much more than we do these days. Since the advent of the printing press, and especially with the invention of the mobile phone, we don't have to rely on our own memories in the same way today. If we forget, we can just 'Google it'. These writers and the eyewitnesses would have been much better at remembering details than we are. Some cultures in the world are still much better at this than others. I was always amazed and impressed at my Asian friends' superior ability to recall factual details for an exam. It is also reasonable to suppose that some would have made written notes during Jesus' lifetime. It certainly wasn't the case that everyone was illiterate.[12]

Another reason why the accounts weren't written earlier may be that the eyewitnesses were too busy *telling* people verbally. But as they grew older, there was a greater need to record the details for subsequent generations. The same has happened recently, with numerous books being written about the Holocaust before the eyewitnesses die. It may also be the case that just as Paul wrote letters to churches he could not visit, so Gospel writers may have written for people beyond their physical reach.

It's also worth knowing that, when compared with other figures from history, the evidence for Jesus does surprisingly well. For instance, with Alexander the Great, despite there being coins from his time bearing his name, the earliest complete surviving account of his life is from 400 years after his death.[13] It was not uncommon for Roman historians to write about events that took place hundreds of years before.[14]

Weren't the Gospels biased?

Another reason people cite for not considering the Gospels as real history is that they are not neutral sources. Each of the authors had become a follower of Jesus, and wrote with the hope that others would follow him as well.

It is true that the Gospels are not neutral. It's impossible to be impartial when you consider the magnitude of Jesus' claims. However, this doesn't mean we should dismiss the Gospels as not being historical sources. Far from it! Complete neutrality in *any* area of history is impossible. Yet, just because people have motives for writing and opinions of their own, it doesn't mean that we should discount everything they say.[15] For instance, two newspapers may have very different opinions about the last general election. We may doubt the neutrality of their opinion, but we would be in no doubt about the fact that there had been an election, or what the result had been. We should, rightly, take people's motives into account, but that doesn't stop us discovering truth.

It is interesting to turn the question around and ask, 'Why would the Gospel writers have written their books, had the stories not been true? What would their motive have been?' All of the early Christians faced persecution, and many died for their belief in Jesus. The authors received no benefit politically, socially or economically. In contrast to the growth of Islam, which increased with political power, Christianity grew for 300 years in spite of significant opposition.

People sometimes do make up stories. I myself used to do so to get out of trouble. 'My sister did it!'; 'The rabbit ate it!'; 'It was on fire when I got here!' were some of my excuses. Yet while I often made up stories to get myself out of trouble, I never ever made up a story to get myself into trouble![16] Why would the authors of the Gospels have made up the stories when they would have had to do so at such great cost?

There are very good reasons to treat the Gospels as real historical sources. They are written within a generation and contain eyewitness testimony, and were produced by people who, though not formally educated, were clearly diligent in their work. There is no reason to suggest that they would have

Why would the authors of the Gospels have made up the stories when they would have had to do so at such great cost?

forgotten the details, given the oral culture and the nature of what they were recording. Though not unbiased, the authors' motives were shown to be genuine by their willingness to suffer persecution for those things claimed. But how do we know they didn't invent the stories?

So, how do we know they didn't fabricate the stories?

Is fabricating a gospel as easy it seems? Let's imagine you were trying to fabricate a story today. You can make it up, but it has to sound like it is true. What are some of the challenges that you would face? For a start, what would you call the people in your story? If you were going to make it sound authentic, then you would want the names to reflect the popular names in the era you were writing about. This would be difficult if you were writing about another culture or a previous generation. However, it would still be hard, even if you were writing about your own. Let me explain.

Among males of all ages in the UK today, what do you think are the four most popular names? Have a guess before you turn to the endnote to find out![17]

It's not as easy to guess as you might think. Most people get one or two, but rarely all four, and never in the correct order. However, what if I were to write about a large sample of real people who live in the UK? Then, the names should naturally reflect the national prevalence.

So, I decided to try it out. It wasn't hard to find a large sample of real people. My local church has around 400 members. After some fun with the Members' Directory and a pen, I had calculated that the four most popular male names were exactly the same as the national mode! What was difficult to guess had been revealed, simply by finding some real people. Not content to stop there, I then used my calculator to work out the percentage popularity of the names, and was amazed to discover the following:

In the UK	%	In my church	%
John	9	John	11
David	9	David	9
Michael	6	Michael	7
Paul	5	Paul	4

So, what is very hard to guess is easy to get right when you are writing about real people. New Testament Professor Richard Bauckham has applied this to the names used in the Gospel accounts.

Using the results of recent studies by Israeli scholar Tal Ilan,[18] we can determine the most popular male names in first-century Palestine. What do we find when we look in the Gospels?[19]

Male names in first-century Palestine	In the Gospels and Acts
Simon	Simon
Joseph	Joseph
Lazarus	Judas
Judas	John
John	James

The results are striking, especially given that the sample of names in the Gospels is far smaller than the number of members in my local church. When we look at some percentages, we see another remarkable similarity.[20]

Male names in first-century Palestine	Male Jewish names in the Gospels and Acts
15.6% bore one of the two most popular names – Joseph or Simon	18.2% bore one of the two most popular names – Joseph or Simon
41.5% bore one of the nine most popular names	40.3% bore one of the nine most popular names
7.9% bore a name attested only once in the other sources	3.9% bore a name attested only once in the other sources

'Yes, but that doesn't prove that the Bible is true!' responded one student as I explained this, and, of course, he's right. It doesn't prove it. But it does show how, in an area that would be very easy to get wrong, the Gospel writers got it right. Remember too that access to data and statistics would have been much more challenging for them than it is for us. I can easily find the names of people in previous generations and cultures by using the Internet. Richard Bauckham comments, 'These features of the New Testament data would be difficult to explain as the result of random invention of names within [the culture], and impossible to explain as the result of such invention outside [it].'[21] The changing fashion in names is well illustrated by the memorial stone for an eighteenth-century woman in Wells Abbey – she was named Saccharina. A modern novelist who called a character by that name in the twenty-first century would be mocked.

This also relates back to the earlier question of accuracy in recalling events that had happened decades before. Try to recall the last film you watched. How many of the names of the characters can you remember? Probably very few . . . but does that mean you can't remember the film? Of course not! It's easy to forget names, but much harder to forget the story. So, if the Gospel writers remembered the names correctly, it gives us great confidence that they also correctly remembered the events as well.

We can apply similar tests to other aspects of the Gospels. How do the authors fare in describing the politics, people, geography, botany, architecture and customs of the place and time about which they are writing? Again and again, we see that they get this correct. This is harder than you might imagine, given that less than forty years after Jesus, Jerusalem was destroyed by the Romans and was never the same again. It would have been hard to invent things later.

Often, scepticism has had to give way, as new discoveries confirm the accuracy of what the Gospels say. For instance, John's Gospel describes a healing at the Pool of Bethesda, which was described in detail as having 'five covered colonnades'. No such pool had been found, and the description of its shape seemed unlikely, so some thought that John must have fabricated it. That was until they discovered the pool! Numerous discoveries reveal the location of other biblical places, such as Nazareth (some scholars had doubted there was such a place); the existence of people, as in an inscription to Pontius Pilate; customs, like crucifixion. There are countless ways in which it would have been very easy for the Gospel writers to have got it wrong, had they been making the detail up. Repeatedly, they are shown to have got it right.

Either the authors of the Gospels were the most incredibly intelligent and advanced fraudsters in history or they were, as they claimed to be, ordinary individuals recording eyewitness testimony about people who actually lived, and events that actually happened. It's not so easy to dismiss the Gospels as fabrications when you stop to think about what fabrications would have involved.

If the events really happened, then why aren't there more sources?

If the events in the Gospels really did take place, then why is there not more evidence for them outside the Bible? Why are we limited only to passing references in a few historical sources?

The first thing that can be said is that there is a real possibility that there *are* other sources mentioning Jesus, but they haven't yet been found, or have been lost. This is true of many works from antiquity. For example, take the Roman historian Suetonius. Only one of his works has survived in full[22] (and in it he mentions Christ). We have three more partial works by him, but we know of at least thirteen more that have been lost.

Alan Millard, Emeritus Rankin Professor of Hebrew and Ancient Semitic Languages at the University of Liverpool, comments,

> Any documents written in Palestine, such as reports of the trial before Festus, will have been destroyed or have decayed long ago. Only in unusual circumstances do papyrus, leather or wooden writing materials survive, where they are dehydrated, like the Dead Sea Scrolls and Egyptian papyri, or sealed in anaerobic deposits, like the wooden tablets at Vindolanda on Hadrian's Wall.

There are also reasons why other historians wouldn't be expected to have written about Jesus. Palestine was something of a backwater during the Roman Empire, and any events that took place there were much less likely to be reported. Even in our time an event in London is far more likely to make the news than one in the Western Isles of Scotland.

Perhaps even more importantly, just as the Gospel writers had reasons to share the stories about Jesus, the Jewish and Roman authorities had equally good reasons for wanting to keep them quiet. They were keen to suppress the growth of Christianity, not to advance it. They only referred to Jesus as his influence affected other things that were of interest to them – though in so doing they often let slip more than they might have intended.[23] Given all this, we shouldn't necessarily expect there to be more sources for Jesus. Far from being disappointed, Roman historians would be extremely excited to have not one but four sources so close to the event in question. It's easy to complain about the evidence we *don't* have, but the question is: what are we going to do with the evidence we *do* have?

A powerful silence

The evidence we *don't* have is also a compelling reason to have confidence in the Gospel accounts. It is not insignificant that there is a total lack of contradictory evidence about Jesus from the time immediately after him. If the Gospels were made up, why then didn't someone point this out? Fabricated stories about the kind of public miracles we read about in the Gospels would have been easy to dismiss.

Imagine if I wrote an article about my friend Jon and got it published in the *Daily Echo*. But instead of just telling the truth – that Jon is a landscape architect, keen cyclist and husband to Alex – I made up some more exciting stories. I wrote about how he could walk across Poole Bay without getting wet, how he went into the local hospital and started healing everyone, and how each day he fed the entire population of Poole town centre with the contents of his packed lunch.

Now, the chances of my getting this published are minimal. The chances of anyone believing it are even lower. Some readers will know Jon, and while he is indeed a great guy, they know he can't do any of these things. Yet, imagine if, for some inexplicable reason, thousands of people started believing that the stories were true. Wouldn't you expect that at least someone would point out the truth?

Why is it that no-one in the first century seems to have been able to come up with an alternative explanation for these very public events that are recorded in the Gospels? Was it that they couldn't, because too many people at the time knew what had happened? The events were too public to dismiss easily.

But you can't verify all the events of the Gospels!

We have seen that there are various ways to check that the Gospel accounts were not simply made up. However, it is clearly not possible to find external verification for all the claims they make. Should we believe only what we can check by other sources?

Imagine that my friend comes for dinner. He turns up a little bit late and explains that he had to pop to the shops on the way. What if I were to respond by saying, 'Prove it! Show me a receipt – I won't believe it unless you do'? You would seriously question our friendship if I were to respond in such a way. I don't need Jon to verify everything he says, because he has shown himself in so many other ways to be trustworthy.

Yet this is exactly what many people do with the Gospels. Like the author of the *National Geographic* article, they will only believe them if they can check every detail. However, the many ways in which I can check the Gospels show me that they are reliable and give me good reason to trust them in the areas in which I can't. Ultimately, if I can trust what the Gospel writers say about the biggest event of all – the resurrection (we'll look at the evidence in chapter 10) – then I would find it much easier to trust them in the smaller things too.

External evidence can be helpful in giving us confidence in trusting the Gospels. However, if we are only going to believe what we can verify externally, and dismiss all the other testimonies of eyewitnesses, then we are going to limit severely what we can know not only about Jesus, but also about *anything* in history. Richard Bauckham says,

> This approach is seriously faulty precisely as a historical method. It can only result in a misleadingly minimal collection of uninteresting facts about a historical figure stripped of any real significance. Neither in this nor in countless other cases of historical testimony can the historian verify everything. Testimony asked to be trusted.[24]

If not . . . then what?

Let's pretend for a minute that somehow the authors of the Gospels *did* make up the stories about Jesus. One more area of questioning remains: 'What was the "explosion" 2,000 years ago that is still reverberating around the world today? From what other root did the whole Christian movement grow? Who was responsible for the most amazing and revolutionary teaching the world has ever known, and why on earth were they happy to attribute it to someone else?' It's easy to be sceptical until you have to try to think of the alternatives.

'What was the "explosion" 2,000 years ago that is still reverberating around the world today?'

Scratch and see

We have seen that there are very good reasons for taking the Gospels as historical sources, and we can have strong confidence that the stories are not simply fabrications. Yet even if you are still not convinced, wouldn't it be worth looking at them further?

Imagine that as you walk down the road, you come across a lottery scratch card. You are about to pass it by, until you realize that it hasn't yet been scratched. As a good law-abiding citizen, you look around to see if anyone has dropped it, but find no-one. What would you do? You'd scratch it, wouldn't you? Now, what is the chance that it is a winning card? Very minimal. So why would you scratch it? Because there is still a *chance* it could be the winner! In the same way, isn't it worth having a look at one of the Gospels, even if you still think it has only a small chance of being true? If it *is* true, then the implications are massive.

A great place to start would be to actually read one of them. However, it could be a very dangerous thing to do. It's what my friend Dave did when he found a copy of one tucked under the windscreen wiper of his car. Before that he had been an atheist. Later he became the minister of my church.

The Gospels were not fabricated stories, but how do we know that those we have in Bibles today are the same as those originally written? Haven't they been changed?

Further reading

) Paul Barnett, *Is the New Testament Reliable?*, 2nd edn (IVP Academic, 2005)
) Amy Orr-Ewing, *Why Trust the Bible? Answers to 10 Tough Questions* (IVP, 2008)

⟩ Lee Strobel, *The Case for Christ: A Journalist's Personal Investigation of the Evidence for Jesus* (Zondervan, 1998)

⟩⟩ F. F. Bruce, *The New Testament Documents: Are They Reliable?* (IVP, 2000)

⟩⟩ Craig A. Evans, *Fabricating Jesus: How Modern Scholars Distort the Gospels* (IVP, 2008)

⟩⟩ C. S. Lewis, 'Modern Theology and Biblical Criticism', in *Fern-seed and Elephants and Other Essays on Christianity* (Fount, 1975), and also available at http://orthodox-web. tripod.com/papers/fern_seed.html.

⟩⟩ Mark D. Roberts, *Can We Trust the Gospels? Investigating the Reliability of Matthew, Mark, Luke, and John* (Crossway, 2007)

⟩⟩⟩ Richard Bauckham, *Jesus and the Eyewitnesses: The Gospels as Eyewitness Testimony* (Eerdmans, 2006)

8. BUT HASN'T THE BIBLE BEEN CHANGED?

The Bible is a product of man, my dear. Not of God . . . Man created it . . . and it has evolved through countless translations, additions, and revisions. History has never had a definitive version of the book . . . The Bible, as we have it today, was collated by the pagan Roman emperor Constantine the Great.[1]

So claims Leigh Teabing in Dan Brown's *The Da Vinci Code*.

'You can't trust the Bible,' one Muslim student told me. 'It's been so corrupted over the last 2,000 years that we don't know what the original said. That's why Allah sent the Quran, and, unlike the Bible, that has never been corrupted.'

The journalist and atheist Christopher Hitchens was equally sceptical about the Bible. He described the New Testament as 'a work of crude carpentry, hammered together long after its purported events, and full of improvised attempts to make things come out right'.[2]

It's not just Muslims and atheists who raise this issue. New Testament scholar Bart Ehrman believes that the Bible we have today has been changed so much that we cannot trust what it says about Jesus. His book *Misquoting Jesus* carries the subtitle: *The Story Behind Who Changed the Bible and Why*. He explains, 'The more that I studied the manuscript tradition of the New Testament, the more I realized just how radically the text had been altered over the years.'[3]

It's easy to see initially why this would seem to be the case. Have you ever played the children's party game 'Chinese Whispers' (or, as the Americans call it, 'Telephone')? One child whispers a message into the ear of the next child, who does the same to the next, until it has been passed around the whole circle. The original message quickly becomes corrupted and is often changed beyond recognition. Didn't the same thing happen to the Bible over 2,000 years, only with the added complication of language translations to contend with? Is there any hope of discovering what was originally written about Jesus?

Just imagine, though, if we could go back around the circle and ask the different children what they'd heard. Then we'd know whether the message had been changed, and where. Then we'd have a much greater chance of knowing what the original message was. In the same way, when we translate the Bible today, it is to the earliest manuscripts in the original language that the translators turn.

But how far back can we go?

Two key questions

When assessing the strength of the manuscript tradition of any historical text, there are two important questions that we need to ask:

- *How big is the time gap between the date of writing and our earliest known copy of it?*

No historian would expect to have the original copy of any work from antiquity, so it's no problem that we don't have any of the original Gospels. But is there a large time gap after writing, in which errors that we can't check could have been made? To use the game illustration: how close to the beginning of the circle can we go? Obviously, the closer, the better!

- *How many copies of it do we have?*
  Clearly, the more we have, the better. This means we can check them against each other to see if changes have occurred.

We could apply this to any text. As an example, let's take another historical work from the same period: Josephus's *The Jewish War*, written around AD 75. Our first copy dates from the fifth century, and, in total, we have nine copies. This is fairly typical for works from antiquity and isn't seen as a great problem – historians are content that the manuscript tradition reflects what Josephus actually wrote.

So, how does the New Testament fare by comparison? As a collection of twenty-seven books, they were written at various points between AD 50 and AD 100. Our earliest copy of a part of the New Testament is a fragment of John chapter 18 that dates from somewhere between AD 125 and AD 150. (If you ever visit Manchester, England, then pop into the John Rylands Library where you can see it on display.) Within the next hundred years we have manuscripts that contain all of the Gospels and much of the rest of the New Testament. Over the next few centuries we have 5,000 manuscripts of all or part of the New Testament, in Greek alone.

In comparison with Josephus's *The Jewish War* (or indeed any other text from antiquity) this is remarkable. Therefore, if scholars are happy that the manuscript traditions for Josephus's *The Jewish War* are sufficient to investigate what he actually wrote, then we should also be able to do the same with the New Testament. So, what do we find when we actually look at these different manuscripts?

Comparing the manuscripts

What immediately becomes obvious when you compare the manuscripts of the New Testament is that they are not identical. Bart Ehrman makes much of this. He claims that no two manuscripts are the same, and that there are more errors than there are words.[4]

What about the differences?

Ehrman's objection sounds like a pretty serious threat. Can we trust a book that has so many errors? However, are things really as bad as they seem? For a start, his claim itself should make us think: how can there be *more* errors than words? The answer is in the way Ehrman counts the errors. If a mistake was made at some point in the copying process, then every copy that follows it with the same mistake is added as *another* mistake. So, instead of counting one error, he counts many – when they are actually all the *same* error.

Therefore, the issue here is not with the facts, but with the interpretation of them. However, Ehrman makes things sound far worse than they are. He turns the relative strength of the New Testament (the number of manuscripts available to us) into an apparent weakness (the number of errors within them). Obviously, if we had very *few* texts, then we would have far fewer differences. With 5,000 hand-written copies in Greek alone, it doesn't take many differences in each one to produce a large number in total.

Most of the differences are minor and unintentional. For example, the most frequent 'error' in the New Testament is the removal of the Greek letter 'n' (ν) from the end of a word when the next word starts with a vowel – a cosmetic change that makes absolutely no difference to the meaning of the word. A second common 'error' is in the ordering of the words – which in Greek, unlike English, does not change the essence of the sentence.

The very few places where there is significant ambiguity are openly acknowledged in modern translations.[5] It is important to know that no major teaching of Christianity rests on the particular reading of a single verse in any case. Rather, it rests on the weight of the teaching of the whole New Testament.

Fortuitously, the presence of some differences actually helps to show that there has been no centralized control or suppression by the church. The only time when these manuscripts *were* suppressed was in the early fourth century, but this was due to persecution from the Roman Emperor Diocletian. Thankfully, this suppression wasn't long-lived, and we still have plenty of manuscripts dating from before this time.

We have seen that the differences in the New Testament manuscripts are neither as numerous nor as serious as some may lead us to believe. However, we cannot deny that there are still differences. So, should that make us sceptical about knowing what was originally written?

Can we really know what was originally written?

Despite the various differences between the manuscripts, many scholars are actually confident that we can have a very good idea of the original text of the New Testament. Let me illustrate why.

Imagine a teacher writes a short story on the board at the front of the class, and asks all the pupils to copy it down into their exercise books. Once the teacher has rubbed the board clean, we have lost the original – all we have are the copies. If I was now to enter the classroom and take just one of the copies and read it, I would have no idea how correctly the child had copied the text from the board. For all I know, he could have made the whole thing up – there is no way to check. Imagine, though, that instead of reading just one exercise book, I got to compare all thirty. The chances are that no two would be exactly the same (especially if their spelling was as bad as mine). While I would now be more aware of the differences, I would also be in a much better position to work out what was originally written. It would be easy to identify who had made the mistakes, and reconstruct what was originally written.

In the same way, by comparing the many manuscripts of the New Testament, we can see where mistakes have been made, and reconstruct what the original text was. And this is exactly what modern Bible translators do.

Some may object, pointing out that the above illustration is too simplistic. Our manuscripts of the New Testament are not all copies of one original – some are copies of copies. We could then extend the illustration this way.

Imagine that some of the children are off sick on the day the text is written on the board, so they catch up later by copying what their friends had written in their exercise books. When yet more pupils come back a few days later, they do the same, except that some of them copy a copy that was already copied. Now their mistakes will have passed on through the subsequent copies. Yet, even with this added complication, it still shouldn't be too hard to spot who made the mistakes, and where. The repetition of a mistake isn't really a great problem. In this way we can group similar copies together into what historians would call 'manuscript traditions'.

We can therefore be really confident that, despite the apparent differences, the original text of the New Testament is almost all discoverable today, and is what we have represented in our modern translations.

But why isn't it perfect?

I was explaining all of this to a Muslim friend of mine. He interjected, 'Why would God allow it to be changed at all? The Quran has never been corrupted and has been perfectly passed down to us.'

My first clarification was to point out that, as a Christian, I don't worship a perfect book but a perfect person. Small errors in the manuscripts of the Bible are OK; small errors in the person of Jesus would not be.

However, I wanted to go further and to challenge the assumption behind his question: how do we know that the Quran has been perfectly passed down to us today? Do we have evidence for that claim?

The New Testament has been scrutinized by scholars for more than the last 200 years – a discipline exotically called 'textual criticism'. Yet, until recently, very few people had ever attempted critically to examine the manuscripts of the Quran. However, in recent years this has begun to change. The results are intriguing.

A comparison of the manuscripts of the Quran reveals that there *are* actually differences between them. Admittedly, these are minor, and fewer than in the manuscripts of the New Testament, and most are probably unintentional. However, it still calls into question the absolute claim that the text has been perfectly preserved.

Dr Keith Small is Manuscript Consultant to the Bodleian Library at Oxford University. His PhD was on a comparison of the Quran and the New Testament manuscripts. He raises three significant problems with the claim that the Quran has been perfectly preserved:

1. The texts seem almost *too* identical, and far more so than any other work from history. You could argue that this is the intervention of God, or it could raise suspicion that there has been some centralized control of the manuscripts. On its own, this would not be conclusive. However . . .
2. There appears to be definite evidence of the suppression of other versions of the Quran in the early years of Islam. This is clearly seen in some palimpsests (manuscripts that have been reused and written over) that reveal older copies of the Quran with some significant differences to the current version. In other places we see text that has been erased and edited to fit today's standardized version.[6] Evidence of change is also plain to see in Jerusalem where the earliest texts of the Quran, found on the Dome of the Rock, differ from the received text.
3. Within Islamic tradition itself there is the acknowledgment of two extensive attempts to standardize the tradition of the Quran.[7]

So, while it may appear that the available manuscripts of the Quran are broadly similar, we still have serious questions about the manuscripts that appear to have been lost. One scholar explained, 'While it may be true that no other work has remained for twelve centuries with so pure a text, it is probably equally true that no other has suffered so drastic a purging.'[8]

A more recent example of this happened in the 1970s when manuscripts of the Quran were discovered in Sana'a, Yemen. There was significant worry that Western scholars might find something detrimental to the teaching concerning the

Quran, so in a letter to the *Yemen Times* the following appeal was made:

> Please ensure that these scholars are not given further access to the documents. Also, please rebury them, or if they are not exact reproductions, please burn them. Allah help us against our enemies.[9]

So, while Dan Brown's claim of deliberate suppression is *not* found in the history of the Bible, it *is* found in the history of the Quran. This is a fairly serious issue for those who claim that there are no errors in it at all.

The implication is that it is now impossible to reconstruct, with any certainty, the original text of the Quran. To illustrate this, go back to the classroom in which we sat a while ago. Imagine if one boy deliberately destroys or changes the other pupils' exercise books. While the remaining versions might be identical, it would now be impossible to reconstruct what was originally written. In the same way, by suppressing variant manuscripts of the Quran, the case for its reliability has not been strengthened, but weakened.

Keith Small concludes,

> The contrast demonstrates that, comparatively, there is much more of a possibility of recovering the earliest [originals] of the New Testament texts . . . than there is of recovering the earliest text forms of the Quran . . . With this in mind, it can be confidently asserted that the original text of the New Testament has been transmitted more accurately than that of the original forms of the Quran.[10]

Therefore, it would seem rather unfair to dismiss the New Testament as corrupted, while holding to the belief that the

Quran has not been so. If we dismiss the New Testament because of the differences in the manuscripts, then we have even greater reason to dismiss the Quran. However, if we accept the Quran, in spite of the issues mentioned, then we would have even greater reasons for also accepting the New Testament.

What about the bits that were left out?

We can have real confidence that the Gospels we have in the Bible today are reliable copies and translations of what was originally written. But can we also be sure these were the same Gospels that were originally accepted by the first Christians? In *The Da Vinci Code* Dan Brown claims that there are hundreds of other gospels that were not included. What about the Gospel of Thomas or the Gospel of Mary? Were they originally accepted, but then rejected later for political reasons by Constantine in the fourth century? How exactly did we end up with the four Gospels we have?

It is true that other 'gospels' were written, though not hundreds. They were not included in the Bible because they were written later, and were not independent sources, but later reflections on the sources we already had. They were not written by Thomas or Mary – the names were used to give them a cloak of respectability. They are simply less reliable sources to discover the historical Jesus.

They show no interest in the life of Jesus and so can hardly be called 'gospels' at all. They contain supposed dialogue, with few details of actual events or places, which, as we saw in chapter 7, are much harder to make up. And where they do record places and names, they show themselves to be far less reliable than the biblical Gospels. However, there has been no 'cover-up', for they are readily available to anyone who wants to buy them.

There is no evidence that these gospels were originally included and then later removed by Constantine. However, we do have good evidence that the biblical Gospels had already been accepted as authoritative and grouped together by at least the middle of the second century.[11]

What happened in the fourth century was simply the official recognition of what was already widely accepted. The reason why this wasn't 'officially' done before Constantine is that there was no 'official' state church before Constantine with the ability to make 'official' statements. There's no reason to believe that the New Testament was doctored for political reasons, or that there is more accurate information about Jesus that has been suppressed.[12]

We can have real confidence that the Gospels we have today have been accurately passed on to us through the thirty or so lifetimes since they were first written.

Don't the Gospels contradict each other?

Even if we discount the later 'gospels' and allow for differences between the manuscripts, it is still clear that the accounts of Jesus are different from each other. For example, in the accounts of the resurrection each of the Gospels records the first visitors to the tomb being women. But while Mark's Gospel names three women, Matthew's names only two and John's mentions only one – Mary, and Luke's doesn't specify a number.

However, the presence of such differences is a strength, not a weakness. In fact, completely identical testimony in a court of law would arouse suspicion of collusion between the witnesses. Differences in testimony aren't necessarily contradictory, but can be complementary. In the example of the resurrection accounts, just because John mentions only Mary going to the tomb, it doesn't mean that he excludes the possibility that other women went along with her. He says that Mary went, but he doesn't say that *only* Mary went. Such differences between the Gospel accounts shouldn't be a reason for doubt, but a cause of greater confidence in the reliability of the testimony they contain.

Why is this confidence important?

I am aware that, for some, the content of this chapter might appear to be rather boring! Why does textual criticism really matter anyway? Who cares about manuscript traditions? Let me share a final illustration.

When checking in for a flight, you are often asked, 'Window or aisle seat?' I always go for the window. There are practical reasons for this – I don't have to get up when other passengers want to use the toilet, and the steward with the trolley can't bash into me while I'm sleeping. But there is another reason too, and that is that I love looking at windows! Plane windows are fascinating – at least triple-glazed, with a lovely coating of plastic, they are neither square nor circular. I could look at windows all day.

OK, I admit it. I don't actually like looking *at* windows at all – but I do like looking *through* them. The purpose of a window is so that you can see what is on the other side. In the same way, the Gospels are a window through which we can see Jesus. Their purpose is not that we simply look at them, but rather that we focus on their subject.

Now, if a window is damaged, we won't be able to see through it properly. The quality of the window affects what we can see. In the same way, the question of the transmission of the Gospels will affect how clearly we can come into contact with the Jesus of history, and what we can see of him.

Our purpose is not simply to study their accuracy, and end there. Rather, we need to look through the window and see Jesus himself. That's exactly what we're going to do now.

Further reading

❭ Paul Barnett, *Is the New Testament Reliable?*, 2nd edn (IVP Academic, 2005)

❭ Michael Green, *The Books the Church Suppressed: Fiction and Truth in* The Da Vinci Code (Monarch, 2012)

❭ Amy Orr-Ewing, *Why Trust the Bible? Answers to 10 Tough Questions* (IVP, 2008)

❭❭ F. F. Bruce, *The New Testament Documents: Are They Reliable?* (IVP, 2000)

❭❭ D. A. Carson and Douglas J. Moo, *An Introduction to the New Testament* (Apollos, 2005), especially chapters 2, 8 and 26

❭❭ Keith E. Small, *Holy Books Have a History: Textual Histories of the New Testament and the Qur'an* (Avant, 2010)

❭❭ Ben Witherington III, *The Gospel Code: Novel Claims about Jesus, Mary Magdalene and Da Vinci* (IVP USA, 2004)

❭❭❭ Richard Bauckham, *Jesus and the Eyewitnesses: The Gospels as Eyewitness Testimony* (Eerdmans, 2006)

❭❭❭ Charles E. Hill, *Who Chose the Gospels? Probing the Great Gospel Conspiracy* (OUP, 2012)

❭❭❭ Bruce M. Metzger, *The Canon of the New Testament: Its Origin, Development, and Significance* (OUP USA, 1997)

❭❭❭ John H. Walton and D. Brent Sandy, *The Lost World of Scripture: Ancient Literary Culture and Biblical Authority* (IVP Academic, 2013)

9. BUT AREN'T THERE MANY DIFFERENT OPINIONS ABOUT WHO JESUS WAS?

Even if you are not religious, there is something deeply fascinating about Jesus. Just from a historical and sociological perspective, he deserves closer investigation. Yet he never wrote a book, travelled far, held political power or owned any material possessions other than the clothes on his back. Despite his early popularity, most of the crowds who once followed him turned away. Even most of his close followers deserted him at his death. Yet within a generation, and despite opposition, his followers had spread across the Roman world, infiltrating the very corridors of power in Rome. Today one third of the world claims to follow him, and our years are dated from his birth.[1]

Who was this man whose footprints have had a bigger impression on the history of our planet than any other? Opinions about Jesus abound.

First, there is *gentle Jesus, meek and mild*, often pictured in a large white nightie with a blue sash, holding a child in one arm and a lamb in the other. In contrast, you have *religious*

Jesus of the stained-glass windows, austere and unsmiling, with a large golden plate behind his head. *Moral teacher Jesus* will tell you how to live, whereas *liberal Jesus* doesn't care how you live – do what you like, for it is all OK with him. Then there is *political Jesus*, who very conveniently always seems to share the political convictions of the person who believes in him. Some believe in *married Jesus*, just an ordinary man who had children by his wife Mary Magdalene. Others believe in *prophet Jesus*, a great religious leader who pointed forward to an even greater prophet still to come. Then there's *super Jesus* of television fame. He will give you whatever you want: a big house, a big car or a big wife. You just need to 'name it and claim it' (and send some money to the preacher), and hey presto, you'll have it.

When talking about Christianity, I often hear people say, 'I like to think of Jesus as . . .' This always strikes me as rather strange. Imagine saying that of any other figure from history: 'I like to think of Winston Churchill as . . .' Surely the significance is not what we like to think, but who they actually were?

The issue with so many of these 'Jesuses' is that they reveal more about the person who believes in them than they do about Jesus himself. With so many different ideas about Jesus, we might wonder whether it is even possible to discover which is genuine – if any.

Back to the original

A few years ago in Northern Spain an eighty-two-year-old artist made the headlines by attempting to restore a 100-year-old painting of Jesus that had started to flake away. Unfortunately, Cecilia Giménez's artistic ability wasn't great, and the result bore more resemblance to an ape than to the founder of the Christian faith. The work subsequently became known as 'The Monkey Jesus'. Ironically, press coverage led to so many new visitors to the area that a low-cost airline even started flights to a nearby airport!

A similar thing has happened throughout history as theologians have 'monkeyed around' with Jesus, adding their own ideas. The result has meant that the Jesus of tradition has become very distinct from the Jesus of history. We need to strip away the centuries of mutations and get back to the original Jesus.

> *We need to strip away the centuries of mutations and get back to the original Jesus.*

The good news is that we can do exactly that. As we have seen in chapters 7 and 8, we can get back to the eyewitness accounts of Jesus to see what they reveal about him. And what we find there is someone utterly surprising and totally unique.

His popularity

There have been many popular figures throughout history, but few with such a broad appeal as Jesus. Both the religious and the irreligious were drawn to him. We find him conversing just as easily with a respected religious leader as with an immoral woman from a foreign nation. He broke down the cultural, ethnic and religious barriers of his day. His own group of twelve followers included a religious zealot (someone who tried to kill the Romans), as well as a tax collector (someone who had colluded with the Romans). Men and women – religious and irreligious, Jew and Gentile, young and old – all found something fascinating about Jesus. And his appeal is similarly broad-ranging today.

His teaching

Despite the passing of 2,000 years, Jesus' teaching was such that it still forms part of our language today. Phrases like 'go the extra mile'[2] and 'turn the other cheek'[3] originate from him. His teaching astonished people because it was original and authoritative.[4]

Moreover, his teaching was surprising and subversive. He taught that we should love our enemies, do good to those who persecute us[5] and forgive without reserve.[6] It went beyond external actions and challenged our internal attitudes. He didn't just teach that murder is wrong (most people can avoid that), but so is anger.[7] Similarly, it is not just adultery that is harmful, but also the lust that can lead to it.[8] The English writer G. K. Chesterton commented that the teaching of Jesus 'has not been tried and found wanting; it has been found difficult and left untried'.[9]

His character

We are all too familiar with discovering moral lapses in our heroes. There seems to be an almost daily revelation of some new sexual abuse, affair, racist attitude or incident of dishonesty in the life of some previously respected individual. We get used to people who don't live up to their own teaching and standards.

Yet with Jesus we don't simply find someone who taught the highest standards, but someone who lived up to them. He didn't just teach that you should love your enemies, but, astonishingly, he willingly forgave those who crucified him.[10] Jesus was willing to touch the leper,[11] to help those in need, even when he himself was exhausted and in need of rest.[12] He dignified women by including them among his followers, accepting their support,[13] teaching them[14] (something Jewish rabbis did not do) and using them as positive examples in his teaching.[15]

At his trial he asked, 'Who can accuse me of wrong?'[16] Not even his enemies could. Most of us wouldn't need to go further than our friends to find someone willing to do so! Despite the efforts of many, no accusation thrown at Jesus could hold. Muhammad is recorded as praying seventy times a day for forgiveness.[17] Yet, despite teaching others to pray for forgiveness,[18] Jesus never asked for it himself. And he didn't need to.

His lifestyle and attitude

Despite being the founder of the world's largest religion, Jesus was surprisingly distinct from what we expect of a religious leader. He went to parties,[19] enjoyed good food and turned water into wine.[20] The religious authorities accused him of being 'a glutton and a drunkard'[21] – not an accusation that you'd normally expect to be made of a religious leader. They simply couldn't understand why he kept going for dinner with the 'undesirables' of society.[22]

Jesus neither condemned nor condoned those who were aware of their own failings. His strongest words were reserved for the religious who seemed blind to their own mistakes and acted as if they were morally superior.[23] He condemned hypocrisy and legalism in the strongest terms – unafraid of upsetting the religious elite. On at least one occasion he went into a place of worship and turned the place upside-down – so outraged was he to find people using religion to make money.[24]

I find it ironic that people tell me that they reject Christianity because they hate religious hypocrisy, when the person who founded Christianity hated it even more.

The atheist journalist Matthew Parris wrote in *The Spectator*, 'One of the reasons we can be almost certain that Jesus really existed is that if He had not, the Church would never have invented Him.'[25]

His fulfilment of prophecy

It seems that many famous people today are getting their biographies written earlier and earlier. A footballer reveals the story of his life by the age of twenty-five. A pop star is in print before she has even finished her teenage years. Yet Jesus has the unique acclaim of having his biography written *before* he was even born!

The Old Testament part of the Bible contains numerous prophecies that were written hundreds of years before Jesus, and yet were remarkably fulfilled in his life. The details of his birth, upbringing, life and death are predicted, long before they ever took place.[26] It has been calculated that the chances of one person fulfilling just eight of the Old Testament prophecies would be 1 in 10. To picture the probability of this, imagine covering the whole of England four feet deep in one-pence pieces – one of which is painted blue. Then parachute a blind man into the country and see if he randomly picks that blue coin at his first attempt.[27]

Several accusations are normally made at this point. The first is to suggest that maybe the prophecies were written retrospectively – after the event. However, the evidence doesn't allow for this. The discovery of the Dead Sea Scrolls in 1947 revealed several Old Testament books, including a complete copy of Isaiah (one of the books with the most messianic prophecies). These were dated from the first or second century BC. It is also important to remember that the Jewish authorities would have strongly opposed any attempt to edit their own scriptures in favour of Jesus.

Another charge is that Jesus, being aware of the prophecies, deliberately lived in such a way as to attempt to fulfil them. While this may have been possible in some instances, most would have been impossible to engineer. You don't get a choice over where you are born, and it's similarly difficult to arrange the details of your own arrest and execution.

Many simply dismiss prophecy, as they would miracles, as impossible. If God does not exist, then of course prophecy would be impossible. However, just as we shouldn't reject the evidence for miracles on the prior assumption that they *can't* happen, so too we shouldn't reject the evidence for prophecy. What if God does exist? Then it is quite possible that it could occur.

His claims

I was sitting in a café in my home town, chatting to a French student. We got on to talking about Jesus, and my friend commented, 'Jesus was just a good man who had some nice ideas.'

'Have you ever looked at any of his ideas?' I enquired.

'How do you mean?' he asked.

'In the Bible,' I explained.

He admitted that he hadn't, so I picked up a copy of John's Gospel and asked him if I could read him one of Jesus' ideas. He agreed, and I began to read the following words, spoken by Jesus: 'I am the way and the truth and the life. No one comes to the Father except through me.'[28]

As I read, the expression on his face turned to one of shock, and his mouth dropped open.

'Jesus was not a good man!' he exclaimed. 'Jesus was a very arrogant man to say something like that!'

'Exactly!' I agreed. 'If he was making this stuff up, then Jesus was one of the most arrogant men who has ever lived!'

Jesus didn't just claim to know the way, or to have found the truth or to offer life. He said he was the embodiment of all these things. We could look at his many other claims too:

- He claimed for himself the name of God from the Old Testament – 'I AM' – and repeatedly used it to refer to himself. The significance wasn't lost on the religious leaders who started plotting how to kill him.
- He claimed that God's words would never pass away . . . and then had the audacity to claim that neither would his.[29]
- He visited a grieving family and had the effrontery to tell them not to worry, because he was the answer to death.[30]
- He taught others not to judge, yet claimed that he would one day judge the world.[31]
- He accepted people's worship on more than one occasion. Now, if you were to fall at my feet and cry, 'My Lord and my God!', I might say that you had overstated things a little. When one of Jesus' followers did just that, at his feet, Jesus rebuked him not for saying it, but for being *so slow* to say it![32]

The difficulty with relegating Jesus to the status of 'just a good man' is that his claims are so huge that they don't allow for it. It's the one thing we *can't* say.

His abilities

It's one thing to make amazing claims, but quite another thing to back them up. I could walk into the centre of my town and proclaim that I am the way, the truth and the life – it doesn't mean that I am, or that anyone will believe me. They are more likely to suggest that I have discharged myself from the local psychiatric hospital. So, how could you convince people to believe such incredible claims?

Jesus anticipates this very issue. On one occasion he was at home, teaching, and such a large crowd had gathered that there was no way anyone else could get in through the door.[33]

So, when four friends came, bringing a paralysed man, they used their ingenuity and went in through the roof. Digging through the mud, they lowered their friend down into the centre of the room. Once the dust had settled, Jesus looked at the man and declared, 'Son, your sins are forgiven.' This must have surprised everyone – they were expecting a healing! It also enraged the religious leaders, who started talking among themselves, 'How could he claim to forgive sin? Only God can do that!'

Jesus then asked them a rhetorical question: 'Which is easier: to say to this paralysed man, "Your sins are forgiven," or to say, "Get up, take your mat and walk"?' On the surface, the former is much easier. Anyone can *claim* to forgive sin – there's no objective way of knowing whether they really have. Jesus continues, '". . . I want you to know that the Son of Man has authority on earth to forgive sins." So he said to the man, "I tell you, get up, take your mat and go home."' Jesus backs up his invisible claim with a very visible action.

Jesus not only says the kind of things that God alone could say; he also does the kind of things that God alone could do.

Jesus not only says the kind of things that God alone could say; he also does the kind of things that God alone could do. On another occasion, he says that if we can't believe on the basis of what he *says*, then we should be able to on the basis of what he *does*.[34]

Throughout the Gospels we see Jesus' remarkable abilities. He frequently heals the sick – in a much more profound way than 'faith-healers' claim to do today. He was able to make the blind see,[35] the deaf hear and the mute speak.[36] He had the power to set people free from enslaving forces of evil.[37] With just a packed lunch, he could feed a crowd big enough to fill a football stadium.[38] He had the ability to calm a raging storm with just a word.[39] Most remarkably of all, though, not even death was beyond his power – he could raise others back to life, and he himself would not be held captive by it.[40]

Many will try to dismiss such miracles as impossibilities, but, as we have already seen in chapter 6, this is a mistake. Of course, not all the miracles of Jesus are as easy to verify – some were witnessed by only a few. Yet many others were very public and undeniable. In the next chapter we'll look at the biggest miracle of all, the resurrection. If we find that there is compelling evidence that this event took place, then it is not at all unreasonable to conclude that the others did as well.

On several occasions, after witnessing Jesus' remarkable abilities, his followers asked the same astonished question: 'Who is this?'[41]

The settled answer that they eventually came to was this: in Jesus of Nazareth, God himself had come into human history.

They reasoned that Jesus couldn't be merely a prophet, or simply a great teacher, or just an enlightened figure. The only thing that could explain both the actions and the claims of Jesus was that God himself had come.

How can you *really* believe that Jesus was God?

I'm aware that such a conclusion may raise several big objections in your mind. Let's have a look at some of them.

The term 'Son of God' or 'Christ' doesn't have to be equated with God

The term 'Son of God' or 'Christ' doesn't have to be equated with God. Absolutely! For this reason, I have not used either term as an argument here. Christians did not realize that Jesus was God *because they thought he was* the Messiah;[42] rather, they discovered that God had *come to be* the Messiah. Two strands of prophecy – one of a coming Messiah, and the other of God's in-breaking deliverance – both found their fulfilment in the same man.

Jesus never claimed to be God

If Jesus was God, why didn't he spell it out in as many words? There could be various reasons for this. Claiming to be God was a very dangerous thing to do in a strict monotheistic culture – it could get you killed. In fact, it *did* eventually get him killed. But that wouldn't have been very useful at all if it had happened before Jesus even began his ministry. It is also the case that rather than just *telling* people who he was, Jesus was more interested in *showing* who he was. We remember what we come to discover far better than simply what we are told.

While Jesus may never have uttered the words 'I am God', it doesn't mean that he didn't make it clear. Let me illustrate. As I write this chapter, I'm overlooking the beach in my home town of Bournemouth. About 200 metres offshore there is a line of large yellow buoys parallel to the beach. They mark the boundary of the speed restrictions for boats, and swimming beyond them is unsafe. A few years ago I went swimming with a friend of mine to see who could reach one of the yellow buoys first. However, when we got close, a lifeguard came out to us riding on a jet ski and warned us not to go any further. We had to turn around. Neither of us won.

What if someone was to ask, 'How do you know it was the RNLI lifeguard?' I would say, 'It was obvious! He emerged out of the lifeguard hut, he wore a bright yellow T-shirt with "RNLI" on it, and he drove a bright red and yellow jet ski.'

'Ah,' they say, 'but did he actually *say*, "I am an RNLI lifeguard?"' I would have to admit that he didn't actually say those exact words. 'So,' my friend responds, 'he wasn't actually from the RNLI, was he?' Such a suggestion would be silly. I didn't need him to spell it out – the evidence was obvious.

When we consider what Jesus claimed, and what he did, the implications are abundantly clear. For instance, on one occasion Jesus told a group of religious leaders, 'Before Abraham was born, I am!'[43]

This was a shocking claim, considering that Abraham had been born 2,000 years beforehand, and also because he was using the name of God (I am) to refer to himself. His hearers immediately tried to stone him to death for blasphemy. They understood quite clearly that Jesus was claiming to be God.

Jesus' deity was a later invention

It is common to think that this 'divine Jesus' was an idea that evolved over time. However, there is absolutely nothing to support this. All the earliest evidence shows a clear belief in who Jesus was, in terms of his divinity. As well as the plentiful references in the New Testament, there are also confirmations from other sources. One of the earliest secular references to the Christian church refers to them as 'singing hymns to Christ as to a god'.[44]

Another piece of fascinating evidence was a discovery near the Palatine Hill in Rome, dating from around the third century. It is some ancient graffiti depicting a man worshipping a crucified figure with a donkey's head. Underneath, the scrawled text reads, 'Alexamenos worships his God.'[45] Though designed to mock the early Christians, the graffiti unwittingly reveals a key truth. Even the enemies of Christianity knew that Christians worshipped a person who was crucified, and one whom they believed to be God. Amusingly, it seems that

a Christian, possibly even Alexamenos, sought to get his own back by adding, nearby, the words: 'Alexamenos is faithful'! The divinity of Jesus was no later invention – it was there from the start.

It was easier for them to believe than for us

It might be tempting to think that simple first-century folk found it easier to come to the conclusion that Jesus was God. Such an idea seems too big for an enlightened twenty-first-century atheist, or a devout Muslim. During a conversation recently, a Muslim friend said, 'I simply cannot believe that Jesus was God – that would be impossible to reconcile with what I think God is like.'

However, if there was one culture in history where such an idea was difficult to believe, it was the very culture where it all began. You wouldn't have found stricter monotheists than the Jews of the first century. Their history had shown them the painful consequences of idolatry. They would not easily have come to a belief that a human being could be God – especially when that person had been shamefully crucified by their enemies. The Gospel accounts show us the struggle they went through to reconcile the evidence in front of them with their own preconceptions of who the Messiah should be. Ultimately, they didn't believe it because it was easy, but rather because there was no other reasonable alternative. This should encourage us not to give up, if at first we find these claims difficult to comprehend. We are not alone.

It is also worth remembering that believing that Jesus is God *is* incompatible with the teachings of many religions, and also with atheism, but we shouldn't just accept things only if they fit with our existing beliefs. Rather, we should be willing to change our existing beliefs if there is good evidence to do so.

We must also remember that if we are going to reject the persuasion that Jesus was God, then we have to ask, 'What other conclusion are we going to come to? How else can we explain the evidence that we have examined?'

Was Jesus lying when he made the claims, or was he deluded? Either way, how would we then explain his otherwise exemplary character and teaching, and where then did his unique abilities come from? If we reject Jesus as God, then the evidence won't allow us still to hold on to him as a good man, much less a prophet. We have to decide.

Jesus' death: the most confusing thing of all

For many people, coming to the conclusion that Jesus is divine is difficult. But if we do come to think that, then it raises an even bigger question: Why on earth would a divine being get himself killed?

Unlike the authors of the average biography, the Gospel writers devote an unusually large proportion of their books to describing the events surrounding his death. In fact, Jesus himself predicted his death in detail several times. On one such occasion he was taken aside and rebuked by one of his followers, Peter. If Jesus was who he claimed to be, then how could his death be part of his plan?[46] Surely someone with the power of Jesus would come and kill the Romans – not get killed by them?

For many today, like Peter, the death of Jesus seems confusing. If he really is God, then why did he die? Is it even possible for such a thing to happen?

However, Jesus had explained that he wasn't going to lose his life (an accident), or take his life (a suicide), but that he would *give* his life (a sacrifice).[47] His death was part of his plan. Rather than being the sad ending to a promising life, it would be the very means by which he would achieve his life's purpose. But how?

Jesus' followers had felt that their biggest problem was external – the Roman opposition under which they lived. In contrast, Jesus repeatedly pointed out that their greatest problem was internal.[48] The Queen expressed this well in her Christmas Day broadcast of 2011 when she said,

> Although we are capable of great acts of kindness, history teaches us that we sometimes need saving from ourselves – from our recklessness or our greed. God sent into the world a unique person – neither a philosopher nor a general, important though they are, but a Saviour, with the power to forgive.[49]

Jesus hadn't simply come to teach us how to live. Alone, that would crush us, for we could never match his perfect example. Nor had he come simply to change our external circumstances. He had come to change us! He came to live the life we should have lived, and to die the death we should have died. He came not to offer 'karma'– giving us what we deserve; he came to offer 'grace' – giving us what we *don't* deserve. Jesus took personal responsibility for the dark side of human nature. Through his death, he was going to take the ultimate consequences of it, and release us from its power to dominate our lives. Christianity is not about 'good advice', but 'good news' – that is what the word 'gospel' means.

Christianity is not about 'good advice', but 'good news' – that is what the word 'gospel' means.

The end?

His death at the hands of the Romans should have spelt the end of the Jesus movement. How could his followers continue to believe that Jesus was the Messiah after he had been mocked, ridiculed, stripped naked, beaten and tortured, before finally suffering an accursed death? Thousands probably saw his naked corpse hanging outside Jerusalem. He had claimed to be a king, yet the only crown he had ever worn had been a crown of thorns mockingly placed upon his head at his trial. Yet, somehow, it wasn't the end at all.

Within a generation the Jesus movement had spread to the very heart of the Roman Empire. Despite a number of concerted efforts by the Jewish and Roman authorities, seemingly nothing could stop it.

Why didn't the crucifixion stop the new movement dead in its tracks? How did this belief in a crucified Messiah make it to the centre of the Roman Empire within a generation? What had happened to turn things around so spectacularly?

The answer involves an event so momentous that we need to devote the whole of the next chapter to investigating it.

Further reading

❭ Michael Green, *Jesus for Sceptics* (UCCF, 2013)
❭ Nabeel Qureshi, *Seeking Allah, Finding Jesus: A Devout Muslim Encounters Christianity* (Zondervan, 2014)
❭ Lee Strobel, *The Case for Christ: A Journalist's Personal Investigation of the Evidence for Jesus* (Zondervan, 1998)
❭ Tom Wright, *The Original Jesus: The Life and Vision of a Revolutionary* (Eerdmans, 1997)
❭ Philip Yancey, *The Jesus I Never Knew* (Zondervan, 2002)
❭ Ravi Zacharias, *Jesus among Other Gods: The Absolute Claims of the Christian Message* (Thomas Nelson, 2010)
❭❭ Kenneth E. Bailey, *Jesus through Middle Eastern Eyes: Cultural Studies in the Gospels* (SPCK, 2008)
❭❭ Michael F. Bird, Craig A. Evans, Simon Gathercole, Charles E. Hill and Chris Tilling, *How God Became Jesus: The Real Origins of Belief in Jesus' Divine Nature – A Response to Bart Ehrman* (Zondervan, 2014)
❭❭ Craig L. Blomberg, *Jesus and the Gospels: An Introduction and Survey*, 2nd edn (IVP, 2014)
❭❭ Darrell L. Bock, *Jesus According to Scripture: Restoring the Portrait from the Gospels* (Baker Academic, 2009)
❭❭ Gary R. Habermas, *The Historical Jesus: Ancient Evidence for the Life of Christ* (College Press, 1996)
❭❭ Michael J. Wilkins and J. P. Moreland, *Jesus under Fire: Modern Scholarship Reinvents the Historical Jesus* (Zondervan, 1996)
❭❭❭ Richard Swinburne, *Was Jesus God?* (OUP USA, 2010)

10. BUT ISN'T JESUS DEAD AND GONE?

Writing just twenty-five years after the reported event, the Christian leader the apostle Paul wrote these words to a group of Christians in the city of Corinth: 'If Christ has not been raised, your faith is futile.'[1]

The early Christians were unashamed to make the resurrection of Jesus Christ their foundation. Far from being an optional extra, this was the absolute essential. Take away the resurrection, and the whole of Christianity falls down like a pack of cards. If Jesus Christ did not rise from the dead, then close down every church and use the pages of this book for toilet paper, because the whole thing isn't true!

This claim means that the basis of the Christian faith is not a subjective private idea, but an objective public event. The difficulty with investigating the truth claims of most religious systems is that they rely on the former – a philosophy, morality or experience that it is impossible to verify. There's no way you could show that they aren't true – they are not falsifiable. The Christian faith is different: based on an objective event; one can investigate and find out if it is true or false.

Yet for many, this is exactly the problem. How can we believe in something as ridiculous as the resurrection? It is because the claim appears to be so demonstrably false that many won't take Christianity seriously.

That is certainly how Richard Dawkins responded to the claim of the resurrection when it was raised at the end of a public debate with fellow Oxford professor John Lennox. He mockingly retorted,

> Yes, well that conclusion rather gives the game away, doesn't it? And all that stuff about science and physics . . . What it really comes down to [is] the resurrection of Jesus . . . It is so petty; it is so trivial; it's so local; it's so earthbound; it's so unworthy of the universe.[2]

Dawkins is not alone in his ridicule of the resurrection. Two thousand years before, in the city of Athens, the apostle Paul had declared the resurrection of Jesus before a crowd of philosophers. We are told, 'When they heard about the resurrection of the dead, some of them sneered.'[3]

The problem with mocking someone you disagree with is that this does not constitute a logical argument. Quite the opposite, it is a logical fallacy! Before we reject the resurrection, it may be worth investigating why so many people have believed it. We cannot dismiss them all as 'crackpots', as some of them are highly intelligent. Yet investigating the evidence seems to be the very thing that many atheists fail to do. In a conversation with John Lennox on the subject of the resurrection broadcast later, Dawkins seemed to be quite unfamiliar with any of the arguments for it (that is, if his incredulity was not just a rhetorical device). Not once in

The God Delusion does he engage with the arguments for the resurrection . . . nor do most atheists in their respective works. It strikes me as slightly strange that in attempting to discount something, you don't attack the strongest argument for it, unless you are only interested in attacking a straw man.

Of course, many may respond by saying that the resurrection is so evidently false that it doesn't merit engagement. The resurrection of Jesus is after all statistically improbable – only once in all of history! It's also medically unrepeatable – we can't try to repeat the feat by crucifying others and bringing them back to life (you'll be glad to know). Yet unlikely as it may seem, the question we need to ask is: 'What is the historical evidence?' After all, history can throw up many improbable events, which are, by nature, unrepeatable. It's when we turn to the historical evidence that we find the claim is perhaps not as ridiculous as it at first appears.

What is the evidence?

It is perhaps not surprising to discover that not all historians believe that Jesus rose from the dead. What is surprising, though, is that even among those who *don't* believe in the resurrection, there is surprising agreement about the central facts around the claim. The disagreement is not over the evidence, but the *interpretation* of the evidence.[4] So, first, we need to ask, what is the evidence upon which even sceptical scholars would generally agree?

Jesus was crucified by the Romans
Not only do all four of the Gospel accounts record the details of Jesus' death by crucifixion, but so do non-Christian historians Josephus and Pliny. Even the highly critical scholar John

Dominic Crossan can state categorically about Jesus, 'That he was crucified is as sure as anything historical can ever be.'[5]

Jesus' tomb was empty

If it had not been for the empty tomb, Christianity could never even have begun. Yet the fact that it did begin in the very city where Jesus' tomb was located is compelling evidence that the tomb must indeed have been empty. It would have been far too easy to stop the whole thing, had it not been.

Indeed, there is no evidence that anyone doubted the empty tomb for the next 150 years. Even the enemies of Christianity unintentionally alluded to the fact that it was empty when they came up with the claim that the disciples had stolen the body.[6] Had it not been empty, there would have been no need for them to account for what had happened to the body.

The account of the empty tomb is further strengthened by the fact that the first witnesses of it were the women. This would be a very surprising detail to invent, given that, according to the Jewish Talmud, 'any evidence a woman [gives] is not valid'.[7] Josephus confirms this when he writes, 'Let not the testimony of women be admitted, on account of the levity and boldness of their sex.'[8] Interestingly, in Luke's account of the resurrection the male disciples did not initially believe the testimony of the women, because 'their words seemed to them like nonsense'.[9] When Paul wrote about the resurrection, he didn't mention the appearances to the women at all. We, of course, know that there is no reason why a woman's testimony should be regarded as less reliable than a man's. However, given the prevalent view of the first century, why would you invent the first witnesses of the biggest event to be those who would not even be regarded as reliable?

Jesus' disciples were convinced that he was alive, and that they had met him

Where can we find out about the disciples' convictions regarding the resurrection? Let's work our way back and see how close to the events we can get.

The first collection of sources would be the Apostolic Fathers, the generation of Christian leaders immediately after the first disciples of Jesus. In their writings around 100 years after the events, they speak frequently of the resurrection, and confirm that the disciples (some of whom had been their own mentors) were eyewitnesses of the resurrected Jesus.

We can, though, go back earlier and encounter in the Gospels the testimonies of the apostles themselves. These describe Jesus' appearances to them. The accounts date to within a generation of Jesus.

Yet it is possible to go back even further still to the letters of the New Testament, which were generally written earlier than the Gospels and are easier to date precisely. One key section on the resurrection comes in the letter from the apostle Paul to the Christians in Corinth. He writes,

> For what I received I passed on to you as of first importance: that Christ died for our sins according to the Scriptures, that he was buried, that he was raised on the third day according to the Scriptures, and that he appeared to Cephas, and then to the Twelve. After that, he appeared to more than five hundred of the brothers and sisters at the same time, most of whom are still living, though some have fallen asleep. Then he appeared to James, then to all the apostles, and last of all he appeared to me also, as to one abnormally born.[10]

How early is this piece of evidence? We can date the letter fairly precisely to AD 53 or 54, less than twenty-five years after the crucifixion in AD 30. We can, though, go back earlier. Paul is reminding his readers of what he had already passed on to them when he was with them in Corinth. We know that Paul visited Corinth in AD 50, so this takes us back four years earlier.

We can go back even earlier. Paul says that he was passing on what he himself had received. It is clear that this statement was part of an early Christian creed – an oral tradition that taught core beliefs of the Christian faith. When did Paul himself learn this? A good case can be made for the fact that he first received it right after his own conversion in AD 32. Even Gerd Lüdemann, one of the most famous sceptics of the resurrection, agrees with this.[11] So, we can trace this belief in the resurrection right back to two years from the very event. In historical terms, this is quite extraordinary. Belief in the resurrection was not a late invention, but the foundation of the Christian movement from the very beginning.

From the start, the early Christians taught that Jesus was raised from the dead. But they didn't just claim it; they sincerely believed it. As we saw earlier, many of the early Christians faced severe persecution and often death for their beliefs. From what we read in other sources, it seems that all three of the named individuals in the above passage (Peter, James and Paul) were executed for their belief in Jesus.[12] If they had invented the idea of the resurrection, why would they have been willing to die for it?

Some might object to this, and observe that many people have died for their beliefs, and yet that doesn't make their beliefs true. Today Islamic terrorists are willing to die for what they believe. Yet, while terrorists may die for their belief in the testimony of others, Peter, James and Paul all died because of their belief in their *own* testimony. Many die for things that aren't true, but no-one dies for things that they *know* aren't true. As has been pointed out, 'Liars make poor martyrs.'[13] Had the apostles invented the story of the resurrection, they themselves would have known that it wasn't true.

Even the most sceptical scholars agree with this. Rudolf Bultmann says that the evidence has 'established the fact that the first disciples came to believe in the resurrection'.[14] Lüdemann concurs when he says, 'It may be taken as historically certain that Peter and the disciples had experiences after Jesus' death in which Jesus appeared to them as the risen Christ.'[15]

The belief in Jesus Christ's resurrection transformed the lives of his followers

Some may try to explain away the fact that Jesus' followers believed in the resurrection as a case of confirmation bias. Did they not *want* to believe Jesus was still alive, as they had staked their lives on following him?

While this could potentially be levelled at Peter, one of the existing disciples, it cannot stand for Paul or for James – the other two named individuals. At the time of the resurrection neither of these individuals wanted it to be true.

Paul had been a persecutor of the Christian movement and had been zealous in his desire to eradicate it. However, a remarkable transformation occurred, and he became a preacher of the very faith that he had previously sought to destroy. What made the difference? He explains that it was an encounter with the risen Jesus.[16]

James was one of the brothers of Jesus. During Jesus' lifetime he had been known as a sceptic who hadn't believed in him.[17] Yet after the resurrection he not only became a follower of Jesus, but he was a leader of the church in Jerusalem up until his execution.

The growth of the Christian movement

After Jesus' crucifixion, his following did not die out, but rather exploded with growth. Starting in the very city where the events had taken place (and where all the evidence was to hand), within a generation, and despite persecution, they had reached Rome, where their presence was noted by the Roman historian Tacitus.[18] At the heart of their teaching was the conviction that Jesus was alive. This was evidenced by the fact that they met together on Sundays – the day of resurrection – a radical departure from Jewish tradition. The two practices of baptism and the Eucharist were, among other things, visible reminders of their belief in the resurrection.[19]

As we have seen, there is surprising agreement on the evidence surrounding the resurrection. Even critical scholars who deny the resurrection generally agree on these facts. Where they differ is in their interpretation of them.

It is worth remembering that different interpretations do not exclude the possibility that one of them might be right. A parent may come home to find a broken window, and very different explanations from each of their children . . . but this doesn't change the fact that the window is broken, nor does it exclude the possibility that one of the children might be telling the truth.

Interpreting the evidence

What we need to do is to examine the explanations, and see which makes most sense of the evidence available.

The story of the resurrection was a legend that grew over time

Legends take time to grow. For instance, the only record of miracles in the life of the Buddha, Siddhartha Gautama, is recorded 500 years after his death, meaning that there should be a healthy degree of scepticism towards them. However, we have seen that belief in the resurrection can be traced back to the original eyewitnesses of Jesus, and to within two years of the events. In any case, legend doesn't explain away the hard fact of the empty tomb or the conviction of the eyewitnesses that Jesus was alive.

The early Christians didn't mean resurrection in a literal sense

Some may suggest that the resurrection was just a metaphorical idea. But there is no evidence that the early Christians thought of it in this way. Would the disciples have died for a metaphor? Would such an idea have changed a sceptic like Paul or James? And again, it doesn't get away from the fact that there was a real empty tomb.

Someone else died on the cross

The Quran says, 'They killed him not, nor crucified him, but so it was made to appear to them . . .'[20] and among Muslims it is generally believed that someone else died on the cross instead. Yet there is absolutely no evidence from the time to support this – the idea originated 600 years later. It would seem very strange indeed that those so keen to secure his death would have made such a basic mistake. There is no reason to think that this could have happened.

Jesus wasn't really dead

Could Jesus have simply passed out on the cross, and been revived in the tomb? It wouldn't be the first time in history that someone had been falsely mistaken for being dead.

Such an idea reveals an ignorance of the process of Roman crucifixion. The scourging beforehand would have brought the victim close to death. The soldiers in charge of the event

164 | BUT IS IT TRUE?

were very experienced at their grim profession, and had a vested interest in doing it right. To check that Jesus was dead, a spear was thrust into his side, and one of the eyewitness reports was that blood and water poured out separately – most probably revealing that the heart itself had been ruptured.[21]

Yet just imagine that somehow, against all the evidence, Jesus hadn't died. We then have to believe that everyone missed the signs of life when they took him off the cross. While suffering from terrible wounds and blood loss, and probably severe shock, he revived in the tomb. He would have had to unravel himself from yards of burial cloth, push away a heavy round stone and evade the Roman guards. He would then need to appear to his disciples and convince them that he wasn't a desperately sick man in need of immediate medical treatment, but rather the resurrected Lord whom they should trust. Anyone who had been crucified would not have been able to walk, let alone achieve that type of feat!

The women went to the wrong tomb

It must immediately be noted at this point that the above is only an argument that I have heard men use! If the women had gone to the wrong tomb, then the men who later went to investigate would also have had to go to the wrong tomb. What is more, you don't easily forget where you have buried a loved one.

This idea also neglects the fact that the empty tomb alone would not have been enough to start the Christian movement. The empty tomb simply left them bewildered and fearful. The encounters with Jesus were also needed in order for it to begin.

It is also worth imagining what would have happened had the disciples indeed gone to the wrong tomb. Peter stood up fifty days later in the same city and declared, 'God has raised this Jesus to life, and we are all witnesses of it.'[22] Someone would have shouted out from the crowd, 'No, he didn't . . . he's still in the tomb. You went to the wrong one, you idiots!' They would have shown them the body, and the disciples would have been the laughing stock of Jerusalem.

The body was moved

If the body had been moved, then the obvious next question is: by whom?

- *Grave robbers?* Why would a grave robber risk his life to break into the guarded tomb of a man who was known to have no earthly possessions, and then leave the only thing of value, the grave clothes, behind?
- *The authorities?* Why would they have done so? If they had, perhaps for safe-keeping, why didn't they produce the body after the resurrection was proclaimed a few weeks later? It is interesting that there is no alternative explanation in the Jewish Talmud. It's also good to remember that neither of these arguments explains the appearances of Jesus to the disciples.
- *The disciples?* The most obvious suspects would be the disciples. This is also the earliest theory circulated by the guards.[23] But were the disciples in a position to do so, or to have been able to? And had they done so, somehow, they would have known that the whole thing was a hoax. Yet we have already seen that they were utterly convinced that Jesus was alive. Why would they maintain their story in the face of persecution? Chuck Colson, imprisoned for his part in the Watergate scandal in the US, explained it well: 'Take it from one who was inside the Watergate web looking out, who saw firsthand

how vulnerable a cover-up is: Nothing less . . . (than the
witness of Someone) . . . as awesome as the resurrected
Christ could have caused those men to maintain to their
dying whispers that Jesus is alive and Lord.'[24]

The disciples were hallucinating

One of the popular explanations today for the disciples' belief
in the resurrection is that they were experiencing hallucinations, brought on by their intense grief following Jesus'
crucifixion. If correct, this would explain why the disciples
were so convinced that Jesus was alive.

I recently stayed with Glynn Harrison, Professor Emeritus
of Psychiatry at Bristol University. I asked him whether he
thought that the resurrection appearances could be explained
away in such a manner. His response was that hallucinations
are 'abnormal sensory perceptions of something not actually
present'. They usually occur in severe mental illness, but can
also occur in other circumstances, such as sensory deprivation
or periods of intense grief.

The hallucinations that sometimes occur during intense
grief have the following features:

- They are usually brief, one-off events, experienced at
  the margins of perception, for example, glimpsing a
  face in a crowd or out of the corner of an eye.
- They are usually experienced in one sensory modality,
  for example, being either heard *or* seen (very rarely
  touch or smell), rather than occurring in several
  modalities at once.
- They can sometimes be more complex in nature, for
  instance, speaking in conversation rather than a brief
  sentence, but this is more characteristic of severe
  mental illness.

So, I asked, could any of these features of hallucinatory experiences explain the resurrection appearances? Glynn's response was this:

> The experiences described in the Gospels don't fit any of these patterns. The resurrection appearances are to large as well as smaller groups of people, involving a wide range of personalities and varying degrees of scepticism. They take place in many different circumstances and locations. The experiences are complex and involve several modalities at the same time (hearing, seeing and touching), and sometimes a period of prolonged interaction. There is nothing to indicate mental illness on the part of all the disciples, and the descriptions of their collective state of mind do not remotely reflect the intense group hypnotic trance-like states that can be worked up by some stage hypnotists.

Hallucinations do not explain away the appearances of Jesus, nor do they account for the empty tomb.

A combination of the above

We have seen that none of the above explanations satisfactorily deals with all the evidence that we outlined at the beginning. Some people may then suggest that a combination of the explanations could account for them. The problem with this is that it still does not deal with the individual flaws that we have seen with each of the above explanations. It would actually dramatically increase the improbability of the explanation, as the probabilities become multiplied together.

Jesus rose from the dead

Unlikely as it seems at first, once we have looked at the evidence, the resurrection is far more plausible than we initially thought. New Testament scholar C. F. D. Moule explained that the evidence 'rips a great hole in history, a hole the size and shape of the Resurrection . . .'[25] Considering the evidence, it's the alternatives to the resurrection that seem implausible and far-fetched. They would require more blind faith.

We saw earlier that David Hume claimed that the only way you could believe in a miracle is if the alternative explanation would be an even bigger miracle. However, we see here that this is exactly what we would need.

> *Considering the evidence, it is the alternatives that would require more faith.*

Some might say that they prefer the miracle of a group hallucination to the miracle of the resurrection. The problem with this is that there was not just one group appearance, but several. So, you would have to appeal to several miraculous events to deny the one miracle of the resurrection! In the light of the evidence, it is the alternatives that would require more faith.

Professor Tom Wright has written extensively on the subject of the resurrection. He concludes, 'The resurrection of Jesus does in fact provide a *sufficient* explanation for the empty tomb and the meetings of Jesus. Having examined all the other possible hypotheses I've read about anywhere in the literature, I think it is also the *necessary* explanation.'[26]

Isn't it just too hard to believe?

Perhaps you still object. It's just too hard for you to believe because it would mean a massive change in your whole worldview. And of course, it would! The resurrection of Jesus is a massive challenge to every belief system, be that atheistic materialism, Islam, Buddhism or whatever. However, it was no less a challenge, and possibly more so, for those in the first century.

The first followers of Jesus didn't come to believe in the resurrection because it was easy or fitted neatly with their beliefs. Tom Wright shows that the Jewish and Greek world-views of the first century were equally as opposed to the idea of the resurrection of Jesus. The Jews believed in one resurrection for everyone at the end of time. The Greeks believed in the immortality of the soul, but not the body. Neither had any concept of the resurrection anything like that which is portrayed in the Gospels.

The initial incredulity of the disciples in the face of mounting evidence is an example of this. Despite Jesus' own prediction of his resurrection, none of them was expecting it. Three days after the crucifixion, the women thought they were going to anoint a dead body. Even on finding the empty tomb, they still didn't 'get it'. When Jesus appeared to them, their immediate reaction was to think that he was a ghost, until he convinced them otherwise. They didn't believe it because it was easy; they believed it because it was true.

So why doesn't everyone believe it?

If the evidence for Jesus' resurrection is so convincing, and the alternatives are so incredible, then why is it that many scholars still don't believe it? Interestingly, the opinion of many is simply to conclude that we just don't know what happened. Is this something they are driven to by a lack of sufficient evidence?

But could it be that it is not the lack of evidence, but the reality of the implications that stops so many of us from reaching a conclusion? After all, if Jesus is alive, then that changes everything, as we will now see.

Further reading

❭ Michael Green, *Man Alive!* (IVP, 1967)

❭ Frank Morison, *Who Moved the Stone?* (Authentic Media, 2006)

❭ Lee Strobel, *The Case for Christ: A Journalist's Personal Investigation of the Evidence for Jesus* (Zondervan, 1998)

❭❭ Gary R. Habermas and Michael Licona, *The Case for the Resurrection of Jesus* (Kregel, 2004)

❭❭ William Lane Craig, *The Son Rises: The Historical Evidence for the Resurrection of Jesus* (Wipf & Stock, 2001)

❭❭ Michael R. Licona, *The Resurrection of Jesus: A New Historiographical Approach* (Apollos, 2010)

❭❭ John Wenham, *Easter Enigma: Are the Resurrection Accounts in Conflict?* (Wipf & Stock, 2005)

❭❭❭ William Lane Craig and J. P. Moreland (eds.), *The Blackwell Companion to Natural Theology* (Wiley-Blackwell, 2012), ch. 11.

❭❭❭ N. T. Wright, *The Resurrection of the Son of God* (SPCK, 2003). For an easier summary of Tom Wright's argument, see his Appendix, in Antony Flew, *There Is a God: How the World's Most Notorious Atheist Changed His Mind* (HarperOne, 2008).

CONCLUSION: SO WHAT IF IT'S TRUE?

Throughout this book we have been asking the question: 'But is it true?' We have seen that there are convincing answers to the big objections levelled at Christianity, and there are good reasons for believing that *it is true*. The case for Christianity is not a single knockdown argument, or a simple soundbite. Rather, it is a cumulative series of reasons that, all together, form a very strong case for believing it.

If the case for Christianity is so strong, then why don't more people believe it? It is not because the evidence is weak, but because the implications are massive.

The truthfulness of some claims is actually inconsequential to my life today. I don't tend to lie awake at night wondering if there really was such a person as King Arthur, or whether there really was a Battle of Hastings in 1066. These things don't change my life, or my future. Yet if there really is a God who not only created the world but is involved in it, that would change everything. So, I would like to finish by asking a question of my own:

So what if it *is* true?

The implications

The future is certain
When the apostle Paul finished speaking to the philosophers of Athens, he concluded his talk by announcing, '[God] has set a day when he will judge the world with justice by the man he has appointed. He has given proof of this to everyone by raising him from the dead.'[1]

Paul links the past event (the resurrection) to the future reality of judgment. The same one who rose from the dead will one day be the judge of history.

The idea that God will judge the world is not a popular one for many. However, if God is the source of all life, yours and mine included, then he has every right to do so. In one sense God's judgment is a good thing. We live in a world where so many people literally get away with murder, and very often justice is never done. God's future judgment of the world assures us that justice will be done. Atheism, by contrast, holds out no such hope.

Yet, while judgment can be a comforting thing, it is also a sobering reality. How would *we* fare in the light of God's perfect justice? We so often fail to live up to our own standards, let alone God's. If we are honest, we have to admit that the problems in our world don't exist simply in some distant country. They are much closer to home – in our country, our city, our home, ourselves. Jesus said that it was from within that the problem of evil comes.[2]

The Russian author Alexander Solzhenitsyn suffered in the Soviet Gulag. It would have been easy for him to point the finger at the evil of others, but he didn't. Instead he wrote,

> If only it were so simple! If only there were evil people somewhere insidiously committing evil deeds, and it were

necessary only to separate them from the rest of us and destroy them. But the line dividing good and evil cuts through the heart of every human being. And who is willing to destroy a piece of his own heart?[3]

The problem is not just with our actions, but with our attitudes. If there really is a God who has given us life, how must he feel if we spend it either explicitly or implicitly ignoring him? We enjoy the gifts that he gives us, but without any reference to him. God's judgment has serious implications for each one of us. However, many people just ignore it, and hope it's not true.

I was caused to think about this a few years ago when I was driving along a dual carriageway. I thought I was being a law-abiding citizen, driving at exactly 70 mph, the speed limit. As I came round a bend in the road, there was a police officer pointing a speed gun at my car. To his right there was a large sign, comprising a red circle and the number 50 in the middle. My heart sank.

However, because I had been travelling at 70 mph, I was soon quite a way past the police officer. I looked in my rear-view mirror, hoping against hope that he hadn't seen me. But I could see that he had already got into his car, turned on the blue flashing lights, and was pulling out to follow me. Despite the fact that I was on my way to speak at a church, I must admit that the first thing that came into my mind was: 'If you floor it, Michael, you can beat him!' Thankfully, the thought only stayed there for a second. Very soon the voice of reason overruled. 'He's already got my number plate,' I realized, 'and even if I beat him for a while, the law will catch up with me eventually. Better to pull over and face up to the consequences now.'

Surely the same could be good advice here too. If Jesus really did rise from the dead and will one day be the judge of history, wouldn't it be better to 'pull over' and think about the consequences now? Blocking out such thoughts and hoping for the best would hardly be a sensible thing to do.

The past can be forgiven

'It's always the same,' one student complained to me. 'You Christians are always telling people how bad they are! It's all so negative!' Maybe you share his frustration after what I have just said. Isn't Christianity meant to be *good* news?

My response to him was to point out that it isn't just the Bible that says there is something wrong with the world. The TV news does the same thing every night. When we listen to our conscience, we might also agree there is something wrong with us too. On this, the Bible only affirms what we already intuitively know, but so often choose to suppress. But the Bible also reveals something else that we would never have imagined.

Despite the fact that we have so often ignored and rejected God, Jesus' coming shows that he has not ignored or rejected us. Although God wasn't responsible for the mess of this world, he has intervened to take responsibility for sorting it out. On the cross Jesus was willing to take the ultimate consequences that we deserve, so that we may not have to. God himself was willing to bear the consequences for what we have done.

Some may object to this, as Richard Dawkins does: 'If God wanted to forgive our sins, why not just forgive them . . .' he asks.[4] However, does anyone 'just forgive'? Forgiveness is always costly. When we forgive, we take upon ourselves the hurt that we would have wanted to give back to the person who has wronged us. In the same way, but on a *far* greater level, God took upon himself the pain of our forgiveness. On the cross he paid to put things right. The resurrection is the equivalent of God's receipt, showing that the payment had been accepted.

Jesus once told a story to illustrate this.[5] There was a father who had two sons. The younger one couldn't wait for his dad to die, so he asked for his inheritance money ahead of time. He packed his bags and left – he only wanted his father's stuff; he didn't want his father. Jesus was illustrating the way in which we live our lives, enjoying God's gifts, but ignoring God. We often live as if he didn't exist.

The boy left home and squandered his new-found wealth on a series of temporarily exciting, but ultimately empty, experiences. Famine hit, the money ran out, and he ended up working in a pigsty. He wanted to go home, but he knew it wasn't that easy. How could he go back after the way he had treated his father? In that culture his actions could have been considered a capital offence. He came up with a plan: he would try to work his way back into the family. He would offer to be a slave and pay his way back. Similarly, we feel that if God does exist, the way to get back to him is to earn it. We naturally think we'll have to become religious, try really hard, and then maybe God will tolerate us.

The son travelled home, growing increasingly nervous as the miles went by. What would his father do? Would he even talk to him? As he came over the brow of the final hill, he could see the town in the distance. As he approached, his heart started to beat faster and faster. Then, suddenly, he saw a small figure running out of the town towards him. At first he couldn't tell who it was, but as he got closer, he realized – it was his dad! However, he still couldn't see the expression on his face. Perhaps he was running out to tell him not even to bother coming into town. But as he got closer, he saw that the look on his father's face was not one of anger, but of compassion. He threw open his arms to embrace his son.

The son started to recite his rehearsed apology, but before he could finish, his father interrupted him. He brought out the best clothing and threw a party. There was no way he was going to be made a slave; he was welcomed back as a son. In the same incredible way, God is willing to take us back, despite the fact that we don't deserve it. He doesn't make us earn our way back into his good books through religious efforts and moral behaviour. He wants to freely welcome us back home.

I was retelling this story recently during a talk I was giving in Serbia. Afterwards, I went to speak to a group of students who had wandered into the café quite by accident but had stayed to listen. One of them was visibly moved, and said to me, with tears in her eyes, 'I'm an atheist, but I never thought that God could be like that! I never realized that he loved *me*.' The staggering truth is that he does – even if we have spent our lives rejecting him.

Perhaps one of your reasons for rejecting God is that you only ever saw him as a distant and dispassionate judge, and you have never realized the depth of his forgiveness and love. One student came up to speak to me after my final talk at their university. He had started the week as a very vocal atheist, but had come along to each talk, and had asked some great questions. 'I am still not sure if God exists,' he admitted, 'but if he is like the God you have described, then I would be a whole lot more open to the idea.'

Today matters

What is your purpose in life? What do you hope to achieve? If there is no God, and death is the end, then there is no ultimate purpose to life. We have come from nothing, and we are going nowhere. I will soon be forgotten like those who have gone before, and all my achievements will count for nothing. Even if I advance society and leave a legacy in the world, ultimately that too will one day be destroyed. As Bertrand Russell concluded, 'Only on the firm foundation of unyielding despair can the soul's habitation henceforth be safely built.'[6]

Some may hope that there is something more beyond death – a heavenly paradise where we might live on in some spiritual realm. But if that's true, then what's the point of life now? Is life just a moral exam that we must pass with sufficient credit to get to the next level?

The resurrection of Jesus shows another way. Life is not pointless – it has come from something, and it is also going somewhere. On the other hand, life is not just a test to pass. The physical resurrection of Jesus from the dead shows that there is a real and physical hope that lies beyond death. The Bible speaks about the renewal of our world and the trans-formation of our bodies.

The physical resurrection of Jesus from the dead shows that there is a real and physical hope that lies beyond death.

What difference does this hope make to my life today? It means that everything matters! Because the resurrection affects everything, then everything must be important. Following Jesus is not simply about being good, going to church and waiting for heaven. All of life now takes on deeper significance and purpose. Everything I do matters. My studies, work and relationships all matter. So does culture, education, society and the environment. Nothing good is going to be lost. Following Jesus does not mean living in detachment from the real world, but getting fully involved in it.

This also leads to a greater enjoyment of life. Our enjoyment of a gift is always greater when we are in relationship with the giver. Our problem in the West is not that we have nothing to be thankful for, but that we have no-one to be thankful to.[7] As C. S. Lewis said, 'Praise not merely expresses but completes the enjoyment.'[8] Knowing the source of life leads to a depth of enjoyment of every good thing that we could never have realized before. So, whether I am swimming in the sea, riding my bike, picking blackberries, making jam, cooking dinner with friends or watching a film – my enjoyment of all of it is enhanced by my gratitude to the One who gave me every good gift.

This also makes a difference when life isn't enjoyable, and suffering becomes a personal reality. Knowing that this life is not all there is means that I can trust God to use even the experiences of suffering for my ultimate good. It doesn't mean that suffering is good in itself – far from it – it is an alien invader in God's good world. But although suffering was not originally part of God's design, it can be part of his purpose now. He can use it to shape our character to reflect more of his. Wonderfully, we can also know that death will not have the last laugh. As Sam says to Frodo in *The Lord of the Rings*, 'It's only a passing thing, this shadow. Even darkness must pass, and when the sun shines, it will shine out all the brighter.'[9] Such a hope for our world is not too good to be true. It's so good because it *is* true!

If Christianity is true, it changes everything.

What will your response be?

AFTERWORD: WHAT NEXT?

As we come to the end, I anticipate that you will have one of three different reactions to what I have written. Whatever your reaction, let me offer some advice on where you could go from here.

'That's rubbish!'

You may think that what I have written is just not true, and dismiss it all as rubbish. You're not satisfied or convinced by what you have read, and you still can't believe any of it.

If that is the case, then let me say thank you for reading thus far! You could have put the book down after chapter 1. (Though if, like some, you read the end of the book first, then I take that back.)

However, before you do, can I gently challenge you that it is not quite as easy as simply dismissing what I have said as rubbish? If you are going to reject God, then what better explanation can you give for the things we have addressed in this book? What is your explanation for:

- your own rational mind that believes that such a thing as truth exists?
- the beginning of the universe?
- the incredible fine-tuning of the universe that makes life possible?
- the reality of non-material things like morality?
- the remarkably reliable eyewitness accounts of Jesus?
- the empty tomb of Jesus?
- the conviction of the first Christians that Jesus was alive?
- the growth of the early Christian movement, against all odds, in the face of persecution?

Your alternative explanations, if you are going to hold them, should be at least as plausible as, and have equal explanatory power to, those you have rejected. Remember, they aren't simply more plausible because they are naturalistic explanations – that's to fall into the error we noted in chapter 5.

Can I also ask, 'Is your reason for rejecting God because you don't think he *exists*, or that you don't think he is *good*?' In a TV interview, atheist Stephen Fry commented, 'Atheism is not just about not believing in God, but supposing he does exist, what kind of God is he?'[1] You'll be aware that I have also written a book by that very title: *What Kind of God?* It seeks to respond to the moral objections that we might have with the character of God. It may be that your questions which I have not answered here are dealt with there.

Finally, are you sure that you yourself are being unbiased when you reject these things? Is your problem that you cannot believe, or that you don't want to believe? Is it the evidence or the implications that are the real stumbling block? There were plenty of people who heard Jesus and saw his miracles, but still did not believe. Though they asked Jesus for more evidence, he refused to give it to them. He knew they had had more than enough to make up their minds, and that lack of evidence wasn't their problem.

Belief in Jesus does not require us to switch off our brains – far from it. But it does require us to swallow our pride – and that's hard!

Can I suggest a few things you can do?

- If you are unconvinced by my arguments on any particular point, then why not check out the further reading for that chapter? This book does not claim to be the final word on any of these topics, and I hope that it is not the final thing you will read on them. For some, this book is already too detailed, but for others it will not seem deep enough. There is much more that could be, and has been, said, in response to each of these questions.
- Be honest about your doubts. This book may not have convinced you, but it may have caused you to doubt some things that you previously believed. It's not just Christians who should think through their doubts – we all should. Don't just sweep them under the carpet. Remember that the truth has nothing to fear from honest questioning.

In your investigation don't just rely on secondary sources for your interest in the Christian faith, such as this book, but look at the primary documents. If you haven't done so already, then get hold of a copy of one of the Gospels and read it for your-self. (If you contact me through my website, moetonline.org, I will gladly send one to you.)

- You could also get to know some Christians, if you don't already know any. I find that many people are very suspicious of Christianity when they first look into it from the outside. This is not surprising, given how the media often portray it. But do your own investigation, and see what you find.
- Finally, you could pray (talk honestly to God). Is it possible for an atheist to pray honestly? Yes! Try the following:

> God, I don't think you exist . . . but if you do, then please show yourself to me. I'm willing to go where the evidence leads, wherever that might be.

Such a prayer doesn't force you to admit what you don't believe, but it does show that you are open to the possibility that there might be a God who could answer it.

'I need to find out more . . .'

Perhaps you are intrigued by what you have read, but not yet convinced. You want to find out more before you make up your mind on these things. This is totally understandable, given that this is such a big decision. There are lots of ways that you can investigate further. Here are some ideas:

- Christianity is not about understanding a theory, but about trusting a person. Get to know Jesus by reading through the Gospels.
- You may find it helpful to go on a course designed to help people investigate Jesus and discover what's involved

in following him. The Alpha Course (alpha.org) and Christianity Explored course (christianityexplored.org) are both run in many locations around the world, and you can visit their websites to find one near you.

- Start to pray. God doesn't wait for us to overcome all our doubts before he will listen to us. Ask him to help you with your remaining questions – he will.

Whatever you do, make sure that you do it. The tyranny of the urgent can so often crowd out the important. If the claims of Jesus have just a chance of being true, then they are very important indeed!

Also, do make sure that 'further investigation' doesn't just become an excuse for inaction. We can always find out more, but the question is: do we know enough? Starting a relationship doesn't end the journey of discovery, but takes it to a whole new level. In the same way, there will always be more to get to know about Jesus, but it's far more exciting when it's done in relationship with him, rather than simply looking in from the outside.

'Yes, but . . .'

It may be that you find yourself increasingly convinced by what you have read. You think this may be true. What's stopping you from getting started?

'I'm not 100% sure'

That's not surprising! We've already seen that there are few things in life that we can prove 100%, but that doesn't stop us making reasonable decisions. If we wait for 100% certainty, we would never take a new job, go to university, get married or make any life-changing decision at all.

On a scale of 0–100% the time for action is when we get past 50%. At that point it would be a smaller step to accept what you now know than it would be to reject it. It would actually take more faith to walk away from it all.

'I've still got doubts'

That's OK! There's nothing wrong with doubts, and you don't need to hide them. Honestly addressed, they can lead to greater confidence, as you discover that there are answers to your remaining questions. God doesn't reject us because of our doubts, but wants to help us with them. Don't allow doubts to stop you. Bring your doubts with you, and ask God to help you in them.

'I don't feel it'

It's important to remember that the Christian faith is not based on subjective feelings that could change with the weather, but on objective facts that don't. So the important question is not 'Do I feel it is true?', but 'Is it true?' Belief starts with your mind – feelings are not unimportant, but they will follow later. Not trusting Jesus until you *feel it first* would be like not getting married until you *feel* married. It's the wrong way round!

'What will others think?'

Following Jesus can mean going against the general flow of society. For some, it is just the risk of being laughed at, but for many others, the consequences can be far greater. However, if something is true, then it is worth following, whatever the cost. Ultimately, the benefits outweigh the cost, and there would be a much greater cost in rejecting it.

'How do I get started?'

There comes a point when we need to do something about

what we now know. If you think that it might be true, then why not begin by talking honestly to God? Perhaps the following prayer may be helpful, though you can put it into your own words:

God, I'm not totally sure about everything, and there is a lot that I don't know. But as far as I know how, I want to start trusting you. Sorry for the way that I often shut you out of my life. Thank you that you haven't rejected me, but you welcome me. Thank you that through Jesus I can know you personally. Please forgive me, come into my life now and take control. I ask in Jesus' name.

Such a prayer is not the end. But it is the end of the beginning. It's the start of a journey that will never end, and can get better every day.

Such a prayer is not the end. But it is the end of the beginning. It's the start of a journey that will never end, and can get better every day.

You will find the following things helpful as you get started:

- *Get into a great read – the Bible.* The centre of Christianity is a person. Getting to know Jesus is what it is all about. You could start by reading one of the Gospels. However, in reality, the whole Bible is about Jesus, and all of it is helpful for us to grow and get to know him better. Reading a bit of it every day is a great place to begin.
- *Talk to God.* Because God is involved in the world, he can also be involved in our lives. Prayer is not a magic formula, but simply a way to bring God into the details

of our lives. Any relationship needs good communication. Spend time talking to God about the things you are learning about Jesus, as well as the things that are happening in your life.

- *Meet up with other Christians.* It's great to have the encouragement of others as we start following Jesus. Living the Christian life was never meant to be a solo activity. Find a lively church that teaches the Bible and where they talk a lot about Jesus.
- *Spread the news.* Good news is worth sharing. If you have found something of value, then it's natural to want to pass it on. Don't be afraid to share what you have discovered about God. You may be the means by which others make the same discovery.

I first met Rob at the back of a crowded lecture room. I had just given the first in a week-long series of lunchtime talks at his university. He had loads of questions off the back of what I had said, and we spent a while chatting them through while munching the leftover sandwiches. He was intrigued by the faith of his housemates, but he also had lots of objections to it.

After our initial conversation, he came back each day, and after each talk we chatted through more of his questions. By the Thursday, he admitted that he didn't have any more objections. So, I left him with a challenge. He had twenty-four hours to think of a good reason why he *shouldn't* become a Christian. The following evening I asked him if he could think of any, and he admitted that he couldn't. 'So how do I get started?' he asked. I replied that it would be good to begin with talking honestly to God and suggested the kind of prayer he could pray, similar to the one above.

Sitting at the back of the crowded atrium that evening, the journey began for Rob. A couple of months later he wrote to me. In his letter he said, 'I'm surprised how quickly things have gone since Events Week, but still I remember a lot of it as though it were yesterday, especially the Friday! But yeah, thank you so much for having the patience to deal with my questions . . . the decision to follow Christ has really been life-changing already.' More recently he wrote, 'It was a big step to pray and give my life to Jesus. It's a step that felt difficult at first, but I haven't looked back since.'

What's stopping you from doing the same?

NOTES

Introduction

1. Dorothy L. Sayers, *Christian Letters to a Post-Christian World* (Eerdmans, 1969), p. 152.
2. The irony of describing Christianity as intolerant is that tolerance itself is one of the fruits of Europe's Christian heritage. Religious tolerance is not found equally in all other parts of the world, nor has it been a mark of those cultures in the last century that tried to establish an atheistic regime.
3. C. S. Lewis, *The Weight of Glory and Other Addresses* (Macmillan, 1980), p. 92.
4. Blaise Pascal, *Pensées*, 414/171, tr. A. J. Krailsheimer (Penguin, 1966), p. 148.
5. Richard Feynman, *Surely You're Joking, Mr. Feynman! Adventures of a Curious Character* (Bantam, 1989), p. 313.
6. Søren Kierkegaard, 'An Eternity in Which to Repent', in Charles E. Moore (ed.), *Provocations: Spiritual Writings of Kierkegaard* (Plough, 1999), p. 47.
7. Daniel Kahneman, *Thinking, Fast and Slow* (Penguin, 2012).
8. Derren Brown, *Tricks of the Mind* (Channel 4, 2007), p. 277.
9. Daniel Kahneman, *Thinking, Fast and Slow* (Penguin, 2012), Kindle edn, Introduction.
10. Ibid., Introduction.

1. But isn't faith irrational?

1. Richard Dawkins, in a lecture at the Edinburgh International Science Festival (December 1994).
2. Richard Dawkins, from the TV documentary series, *The Root of All Evil?* (Channel 4, 2006).
3. A. C. Grayling, *Against All Gods: Six Polemics on Religion and an Essay on Kindness* (Oberon, 2012), pp. 15–16.
4. Mark Twain, *Following the Equator*, vol. 1 (Wildside Press, 1897), p. 114.
5. John 20:29.
6. 'Faith is commitment to belief in something either in the absence of evidence or in the face of countervailing evidence. It is accounted a "theological virtue" precisely for this reason, as the New Testament story of Doubting Thomas is designed to illustrate.' See A. C. Grayling, 'Science and Rationality', in *Thinking of Answers: Questions in the Philosophy of Everyday Life* (Bloomsbury, 2011), p. 112.
7. John 20:30–31.
8. John 14:11.
9. 2 Peter 1:16.
10. Acts 26:25–26.
11. *Premier Christianity* magazine conducted a survey of people's understanding of the word 'faith'. They were asked, 'Do you agree that when Christians use the word "faith" they mean "believing something even though it isn't supported by evidence"?' Of the 700 people who responded, 72% of those who were non-Christians said they agreed with the statement, whereas only 9% of the Christians did: https://www.premierchristianity.com/Past-Issues/2014/October-2014/The-Sceptic-The-Man-who-wants-to-turn-you-into-an-atheist.
12. Francis Collins, *The Language of God: A Scientist Presents Evidence for Belief* (Free Press, 2006), p. 164.
13. See 1 Peter 3:15.

14. The Higgs particle is sometimes also referred to as the 'God particle'. This is a rather misleading title created by media hype. In reality, the Higgs Boson is nothing to do with the evidence for or against the existence of God.

15. Quoted in *The Guardian*, 26 December 2012: http://www.theguardian.com/science/2012/dec/26/peter-higgs-richard-dawkins-fundamentalism.

16. John Gray, *Heresies: Against Progress and Other Illusions* (Granta, 2004), p. 45.

2. But hasn't science buried God?

1. John Cornwell (ed.), *Nature's Imagination: The Frontiers of Scientific Vision* (OUP, 1995), p. 132.

2. C. S. Lewis, *Miracles* (HarperCollins, 2002), p. 169.

3. Quoted in J. H. Tiner, *Johannes Kepler: Giant of Faith and Science* (Mott Media, 1977), p. 197.

4. Psalm 111:2.

5. Richard Dawkins, *The God Delusion* (Bantam, 2006), p. 132.

6. Ibid., p. 159.

7. Colin Russell, *Beliefs and Values in Science Education* (Open University Press, 1995), p. 125.

8. J. W. Draper, *History of the Conflict between Religion and Science* (1881), pp. 6–7: http://www.gutenberg.org/ebooks/1185; Andrew Dickson White, *History of the Warfare of Science with Theology in Christendom* (1896): http://www.gutenberg.org/ebooks/505.

9. Allan Chapman helpfully explains that a fundamental problem with White's book is that 'very often, his exceptions prove the rule. Having, for example, discussed superstitious flat-earth views, he goes on to cite Augustine, Ambrose, Bede, Albertus Magnus, Aquinas, Dante, Vincent of Beauvais, and others who argued that the earth was spherical! Only the most distinguished and influential thinkers of early Christendom, no less – none of whom suffered punishment for their views!' See Allan Chapman,

Slaying the Dragons: Destroying Myths in the History of Science and Faith (Lion Books, 2013), p. 97.

10. Peter Harrison, *The Territories of Science and Religion*, from his Gifford Lectures on Science, Religion and Modernity, University of Edinburgh, 2011: https://www.youtube.com/watch?v=SSzN2t5mAzM.

11. In this particular instance the conflict was not so much between Galileo and the teaching of the Bible, but rather with the generally accepted Aristotelian view of the universe. Contrary to what some have said, Galileo was never tortured by the church, but was put under house arrest (of course, still inexcusable). He probably would have fared much better if he hadn't inferred in some of his writings that the pope was a buffoon! For a more in-depth discussion on this, see Charles Hummel, *The Galileo Connection* (IVP, 1986).

12. Peter Harrison, *Cambridge Companion to Science and Religion* (Cambridge University Press, 2010), p. 4.

13. Results for 1916 and 1996, both studying 1,000 randomly selected scientists. 1916 – 41.8% yes; 41.5% no; 16.7% agnostic. 1996 – 39.6% yes; 45.5% no; 14.9% agnostic. From Larry A. Witham, *Where Darwin Meets the Bible: Creationists and Evolutionists in America* (OUP, 2002), p. 272.

14. Peter Berger at the Faith Angle Forum (November, 2011): http://eppc.org/publications/berger.

15. Stephen Hawking and Leonard Mlodinow, *The Grand Design* (Bantam, 2010), p. 17.

16. Isaac Newton, *Principia Mathematica* (1729), tr. Andrew Motte: https://newtonprojectca.files.wordpress.com/2013/06/newton-general-scholium-1729-english-text-by-motte-a4.pdf, pp. 1–2.

17. From a talk by Professor Thomas Schimmel, Professor of Physics at Karlsruhe Institute of Technology, Germany.

18. Quoted in Denis Alexander and Robert S. White, *Beyond Belief: Science, Faith and Ethical Challenges* (Lion Books, 2004), p. 84.

19. Psalm 98:8.

20. For further investigation into the literary style and purpose of Genesis 1, see John H. Walton, *The Lost World of Genesis One: Ancient Cosmology and the Origins Debate* (IVP, 2009).

21. There has been a great deal of discussion among Christians over their understanding of the early chapters of Genesis in relation to evolution, with many different opinions. For one explanation of how a Christian might reconcile their understanding of evolution with the Bible, see Denis Alexander, *Creation or Evolution: Do We Have to Choose?* (Monarch, 2008). For a different view, see John C. Lennox, *Seven Days That Divide the World* (Zondervan, 2011).

22. Stephen Jay Gould, 'Impeaching a Self-Appointed Judge', *Scientific American*, July 1992, p. 119.

23. Richard Swinburne, *The Existence of God* (OUP, 1991), pp. 135–136.

24. James Ladyman and Don Ross, themselves naturalists, admit, 'However, it does not imply that our everyday or habitual intuitions and cognition are likely to track truths reliably across all domains of inquiry . . . there is no reason to imagine that our habitual intuitions and inferential responses are well designed for science or for metaphysics.' From *Everything Must Go: Metaphysics Naturalized* (OUP, 2008), p. 2.

25. From his letter to W. Graham, dated 3 July 1881: https://www.darwinproject.ac.uk/letter/entry-13230.

26. John Gray, *Black Mass: Apocalyptic Religion and the Death of Utopia* (Penguin, 2008), p. 26.

27. Thomas Nagel, *Mind and Cosmos: Why the Materialist Neo-Darwinian Conception of Nature Is Almost Certainly False* (OUP USA, 2012), p. 20.

28. For a fuller explanation of this argument, see Alvin Plantinga and Michael Tooley, *Knowledge of God* (Wiley-Blackwell, 2008).

29. Bertrand Russell, *Religion and Science* (OUP, 1998), p. 223.

30. John Cornwell (ed.), *Nature's Imagination: The Frontiers of Scientific Vision* (OUP, 1995), p. 132.

31. Stephen Hawking and Leonard Mlodinow, *The Grand Design* (Bantam, 2010), p. 5.

32. This idea is not new. A philosophical movement that gained popularity in the 1930s was called logical positivism. It states that for a sentence to be of any literal sense, it must be either a tautology (a statement of universal logic) or else it must be empirically verifiable. If it fails either of these tests, then the sentence is neither true nor false, but simply meaningless. The fundamental problem with this idea is that it fails its own test, for it cannot be verified empirically, nor is it a statement of universal logic. According to its own principles, the idea itself becomes meaningless. Though popular for a while, the influence of logical positivism declined rapidly within a few years. One of its main proponents, A. J. Ayer, explained that 'the most important' problem 'was that nearly all of it was false'. Quoted in Oswald Hanfling, 'Logical Positivism', *Routledge History of Philosophy* (Routledge, 2003), p. 194.

33. Ludwig Wittgenstein, *Tractatus Logico-Philosophicus* (1922), 6.52: www.gutenberg.org/files/5740/5740-pdf.pdf.

3. But couldn't faith just be a psychological crutch or a social construct?

1. Francis Bacon, *Novum Organum* (1620): http://faculty.cua.edu/mackm/HUM/texts/files/Novum%20Organum.pdf, p. 8.

2. Ludwig Feuerbach, *The Essence of Christianity*, tr. Alexander Loos (Prometheus Books, 1989 [1845]), p. 31.

3. Sigmund Freud, *The Future of an Illusion*, tr. Peter Gay (Norton, 1961), p. 38.

4. Ibid., p. 30.

5. Bruce Hood, *SuperSense* (HarperOne, 2009), Kindle edn, ch. 9.

6. Derren Brown, *Tricks of the Mind* (Channel 4, 2007), p. 13.

7. Richard Dawkins, 'Is Science a Religion?' (Acceptance speech for 1996 Humanist of the Year): http://www.2think.org/Richard_Dawkins_Is_Science_A_Religion.shtml.

8. Thomas Nagel, *The Last Word* (OUP, 1997), p. 130.

9. Aldous Huxley, *Ends and Means*, 3rd edn (Harper and Brothers, 1937), p. 316.

10. Paul Vitz, *Faith of the Fatherless: The Psychology of Atheism* (Spence Publishing Company, 1999), p. 57.

11. *Inception*, science fiction thriller film, directed by Christopher Nolan (2010).

12. Aldous Huxley, *Ends and Means: An Inquiry into the Nature of Ideals and into the Methods Employed for Their Realization*, 3rd edn (Harper and Brothers, 1937), p. 312.

13. Douglas Groothuis, 'Why Truth Matters Most: An Apologetic for Truth-Seeking in Modern Times', *Journal of the Evangelical Theological Society*, 47:3, September 2004: http://www.etsjets.org/files/JETS-PDFs/47/47-3/47-3-pp441-454_JETS.pdf.

14. Bruce Edmonds, 'The Revealed Poverty of the Gene-Meme Analogy – Why Memetics *per se* Has Failed to Produce Substantive Results', *Journal of Memetics*, vol. 9 (2005): http://cfpm.org/jom-emit/2005/vol9/edmonds_b.html.

15. This illustration is taken from C. S. Lewis's essay, 'Bulverism' (1941): http://www.barking-moonbat.com/God_in_the_Dock.html.

16. Peter Boghossian, 'Containment Protocols', in *A Manual for Creating Atheists* (Pitchstone Publishing, 2013), ch. 9. For a discussion of this book, see: http://www.premierchristianradio.com/Shows/Saturday/Unbelievable/Episodes/Peter-Boghossian-vs-Tim-McGrew-A-manual-for-creating-atheists.

17. Nick Spencer, *Atheists: The Origin of the Species* (Bloomsbury, 2014), pp. 214–221.

18. C. S. Lewis, *Mere Christianity* (Fontana, 1952), p. 118.

19. Ecclesiastes 3:11.

20. Augustine, *Confessions*, Book I, Chapter 1 (398), tr. E. B. Pusey: www.gutenberg.org/files/3296/3296-h/3296-h.htm.

21. Blaise Pascal, *Pensées* (1660), tr. W. F. Trotter: http://www.leaderu.com/cyber/books/pensees/pensees.html.

22. See http://www.independent.co.uk/voices/comment/christians-the-worlds-most-persecuted-people-9630774.html.

23. C. S. Lewis, *Surprised by Joy* (Fount, 1977), p. 182.

24. Matthew 16:24–26.

4. But don't you need evidence?

1. Richard Dawkins, *A Devil's Chaplain* (Mariner, 2004), p. 248.

2. Bertrand Russell, *Why I Am Not a Christian* (Simon & Schuster, 1957), p. 7.

3. The problem with an infinite number in reality was communicated by the German mathematician David Hilbert, in an illustration that became known as Hilbert's Hotel. Imagine a hotel that has an infinite number of guests staying at it. Although the hotel is full of an infinite number of guests, you could easily fit another infinite number of guests into it simply by moving the guests – from room 1 to room 2, from room 2 to 4, 3 to 6, and so on. As a result, all the even-numbered rooms are full, but there is an infinite number of odd-numbered rooms that are now empty for another infinite number of guests!

4. Quoted in John C. Lennox, *Gunning for God: Why the New Atheists Are Missing the Target* (Lion Books, 2011), Kindle edn, ch.1.

5. Stephen Hawking, *A Brief History of Time* (Bantam, 1988), p. 46.

6. Stephen Hawking and Leonard Mlodinow, *The Grand Design* (Bantam, 2010), p. 180.

7. C. S. Lewis, *Miracles* (HarperCollins, 2002), p. 93.

8. Lawrence Krauss (2013): *The Flavors of Nothing*: youtube.com/watch?v=UemhCsaeGgc. Cf. his *A Universe from Nothing* (Simon & Schuster, 2012).

9. Astrophysicist Rodney Holder explains, 'Krauss redefines the notion of nothing so that the quantum vacuum can be identified with nothing. This really is a sleight of hand. To philosophers, "nothing" is the absence of anything. The quantum vacuum is a hive of activity with space acted on by quantum fields to produce particles and their anti-particles, and acted on by gravity. "Nothing" seems to be a very complicated something . . .', in Rodney Holder, *Big Bang, Big God* (Lion Books, 2013), p. 71.

10. See http://www.nytimes.com/2012/03/25/books/review/a-universe-from-nothing-by-lawrence-m-krauss.html?pagewanted=all&_r=0.

11. Ibid.

12. Rodney Holder points out twelve examples of fine-tuning that needed to be just right, all of them to an incredibly high degree. If any of these had been different by the tiniest fraction, then the universe would not have been capable of producing life at all. See *Big Bang, Big God* (Lion Books, 2013), pp. 84–99.

13. Paul Davies, *The Goldilocks Enigma: Why Is the Universe Just Right for Life?* (Allen Lane, 2006), p. 3.

14. See Rodney Holder, *Big Bang, Big God* (Lion Books, 2013), p. 93.

15. Paul Davies, *The Cosmic Blueprint: New Discoveries in Nature's Creative Ability to Order the Universe* (Simon & Schuster, 1988), p. 203.

16. Fred Hoyle, 'The Universe: Past and Present Reflections', *Annual Review of Astronomy and Astrophysics*, vol. 20, September 1982, p. 16.

17. From his lecture at the Religious Epistemology Conference, The Royal Institute of Philosophy, 19 June 2015: https://www.youtube.com/watch?v=3Gl_w1yMgCg.

18. John Leslie, *Universes* (Routledge, 1989), pp. 13–14.

19. Andrei Linde, 'The Uniformity and Uniqueness of the Universe', in John Brockman (ed.), *This Idea Must Die: Scientific Theories That Are Blocking Progress* (Harper Perennial, 2015), p. 47.

20. For a fuller discussion about the problems of the multiverse theory, see Rodney Holder, *God, the Multiverse and Everything* (Ashgate Publishing, 2004), ch. 7.

21. John Polkinghorne, *One World: The Interaction of Science and Theology* (SPCK, 1986), p. 80.

22. Ibid., p. 80.

23. David Hume, *A Treatise of Human Nature* (1738), Book III, Part I: www.gutenberg.org/files/4705/4705-h/4705-h.htm.

24. I am indebted to my friend Chris Oldfield for this illustration.

25. https://commons.wikimedia.org/wiki/File:Venus_de_Milo_ Louvre_Ma399_n3.jpg.

26. C. S. Lewis, *Mere Christianity* (Zondervan, 2001), pp. 38–39.

27. Albert Camus, *The Fall* (Penguin, 2006).

28. http://www.telegraph.co.uk/ news/1526206/I-was-in-Hitlers-SS-admits-Günter-Grass.html.

29. Sam Harris, *The Moral Landscape* (Free Press, 2010), p. 39.

30. Another problem with following the logic of Harris's reasoning is that we could argue for the moral goodness of some things that most of us would not regard as 'good' at all. William Lane Craig gives an illustration. Imagine there are only two people left in the world: one man and one woman. If morality is determined by what will maximize well-being for the greatest number of people, then the moral thing to do would be for them to have sex and reproduce. If they don't, then there won't be any well-being for anyone after their generation. But what if one of them doesn't want to? We would normally think that forced sexual intercourse would be extremely immoral, yet according to this theory, it would actually be the only moral thing to do. See http://www.reasonablefaith.org/ is-the-foundation-of-morality-natural-or-supernatural-the-craig-harris.

31. Richard Dawkins, in his book *The God Delusion*, devotes just five pages to it.

5. But isn't Jesus just another myth?

1. Dan Brown, *The Da Vinci Code* (Doubleday, 2003), p. 232.

2. Bill Maher, *Religulous* (2008): https://www.youtube.com/watch?v=FFspMFYntME.

3. *QI*, series D, episode 13 (BBC, 2006): https://www.youtube.com/watch?v=MSm7YPMQOSo.

4. James Fraser, *The Golden Bough* (1890).

5. There is no written evidence for Horus at all, and most of what we know comes from our interpretations of drawings. See James Patrick Holding (ed.), *Shattering the Christ Myth* (Xulon Press, 2008), p. 223.

6. Mithra was originally an ancient Persian deity, but is often confused with the Roman deity of the same name. Although they have the same name, they are actually quite different.

7. It is also worth noting, as Professor Tom Wright states, that 'most Christians in the Western world use the word *resurrection* as a vague word to mean "life after death", which it never did in the ancient world. It was always a very specific term . . .' The idea of resurrection didn't simply imply surviving death or coming back to life again. Rather, it spoke of a new bodily existence beyond death – what Wright called 'life after life death'. For a short summary of Tom Wright's argument, see his appendix in Anthony Flew, *There Is a God* (HarperCollins, 2007), p. 194.

8. The actual date of Jesus' birth is unknown, but many suggest that it was probably not in mid-winter, given that the shepherds were out in the fields.

9. See 1 Corinthians 8; Romans 14.

10. Personal email.

11. Exodus 4:22–23.

12. C. S. Lewis, 'Myth Become Fact', in *God in the Dock* (HarperCollins, 1979), p. 36.

6. But aren't miracles impossible?

1. https://en.wikipedia.org/wiki/Jefferson_Bible.
2. 1 Corinthians 15:14.
3. C. S. Lewis, *Miracles* (HarperCollins, 2002), p. 4.
4. Richard Dawkins, *The God Delusion* (Bantam, 2006), p. 157. Whether or not many Christians feel embarrassed to talk about miracles, it strikes me that the 'argument from embarrassment' is itself embarrassingly weak! It is, in effect, saying, 'Belief X is embarrassing and belief P is not embarrassing, so I choose to believe P.' It is hardly a very solid line of argumentation.
5. David Hume, 'Of Miracles', in *An Enquiry Concerning Human Understanding* (1748): www.gutenberg.org/files/9662/9662-h/9662-h.htm#section10.
6. Nancy Cartwright, 'Is Natural Science "Natural" Enough? A Reply to Philip Allport', *Synthese* 94: 291–301 (1993).
7. Adapted from an illustration used by C. S. Lewis in *Miracles* (HarperCollins, 2002), p. 92.
8. www.whywontgodhealamputees.com.
9. Mark 5:21–43; John 11:1–44.
10. See Luke 4:18.

7. But aren't the accounts of Jesus unreliable?

1. These details are found in the works of Josephus, a Jewish historian; Tacitus, a Roman historian; and Pliny the Younger, a Roman governor.

   Josephus wrote, 'About this time there lived Jesus, a wise man, if indeed one ought to call him a man. For he was one who performed surprising deeds and was a teacher of such people as accept the truth gladly. He won over many Jews and many of the Greeks. He was the Christ. And when, upon the accusation of the principal men among us, Pilate had condemned him to a cross, those who had first come to love him did not cease. He appeared to them spending a third day restored to life, for the prophets of God had foretold these things and a thousand other marvels about him. And the tribe of the Christians, so called after him, has still to this day not disappeared.' (Flavius Josephus, *Antiquities of the Jews*, 18.3.3)

There is some dispute about whether this quote is entirely accurate, as it is uncertain why Josephus would call Jesus 'the Christ' when elsewhere in his writings he says he was not. There is also a query as to why he would infer the resurrection if he were not a Christian. Therefore, some conclude that it is the work of a later interpolator. Even if this were the case, the others parts are generally thought to be authentic, and it is only those parts to which I have referred in my conclusions in the main text. It is worth noting, though, that there is no reason from the manuscripts themselves to doubt the authenticity of the full quotation as it is found in its entirety in all the earliest manuscripts.

His reference to James is also found in *Antiquities of the Jews*, 20.9.1.

Tacitus wrote, 'Christus, from whom the name had its origin, suffered the extreme penalty during the reign of Tiberius at the hands of one of our procurators, Pontius Pilatus, and a most mischievous superstition, thus checked for the moment, again broke out not only in Judea, the first source of the evil, but even in Rome . . .' (*Annals*, book 15, ch. 44).

Pliny's reference to Christians comes in a letter he wrote to the Roman Emperor Trajan, asking for advice about what to do with Christians who refuse to denounce Christ and worship other gods (Pliny, *Letters*, 10.96–97).

2. A term often used by Justin Martyr (second century). For instance, see *Dialogue with Trypho the Jew*, 106.3.

3. Derren Brown, *Tricks of the Mind* (Channel 4, 2007), p. 13.

4. Richard Dawkins, *The God Delusion* (Bantam, 2006), p. 123.

5. http://ngm.nationalgeographic.com/2008/12/herod/mueller-text.

6. Herod slaughtered the last remnants of the Hasmonean dynasty and ordered the execution of his own wife, mother-in-law and several of his sons. As he lay dying, he decreed that all the leading men be assembled in the hippodrome and slaughtered when his death was announced. Compared with that, the elimination of a few babies in Bethlehem would never be headline news.

7. Luke 1:3.

8. Richard Bauckham, *Jesus and the Eyewitnesses: The Gospels as Eyewitness Testimony* (Eerdmans, 2006), pp. 39–66.

9. Paul Barnett dates the letters of Clement, Ignatius and Polycarp in *c* 96, *c* 108 and *c* 110 respectively: see Paul Barnett, *Is the New Testament Reliable?* (IVP Academic, 2003), p. 39.

10. Acts 4:13.

11. Richard Bauckham, *Jesus and the Eyewitnesses* (Eerdmans, 2006), p. 334.

12. For more on this, see Alan Millard, *Reading and Writing in the Time of Jesus* (Bloomsbury, 2004).

13. See Lee Strobel, *The Case for Christ* (Zondervan, 1998), p. 41.

14. If we make some comparisons, the Roman historian Livius (59 BC – AD 17) wrote about events several hundred years before. Tacitus (AD 55–120) sometimes has a similar gap between himself and the events as the authors of the Gospels, but sometimes a much larger one.

15. An example of this is the Jewish historian Flavius Josephus who is open about his own motives in writing. Paul Barnett explains, 'What makes Josephus so interesting is his undoubted ability to provide detailed and factual information *while at the same time* presenting the readers with a sustained "case" against the revolutionaries among his fellow countrymen' (*Is the New Testament Reliable?* IVP Academic, 2003), p. 166. A personal motive in writing does not mean that the source is not useful for discovering truth about history.

16. I am indebted to my former colleague Tom Welton for the idea for this illustration.

17. At the time of writing, the most popular names were John, David, Michael, Paul. How did you get on?

18. Tal Ilan, *Lexicon of Jewish Names in Late Antiquity: Vol. I: Palestine 330 BCE–200 CE*, TSAJ 91 (Mohr Siebeck, 2002), cited in Richard Bauckham, *Jesus and the Eyewitnesses* (Eerdmans, 2006), p. 70.

19. Richard Bauckham, *Jesus and the Eyewitnesses* (Eerdmans, 2006), p. 90.

20. Ibid., pp. 71–72.

21. Ibid., p. 84.

22. Suetonius, *The Twelve Caesars*, AD 121.

23. For instance, Tacitus's purpose in writing was not to show the spread of Christianity, but to explain who was blamed for the fire of Rome. However, in so doing he reveals that Christians must have been a significant proportion of the population of the city of Rome if the emperor could (almost certainly, falsely) fix the blame for the fire upon them.

24. Richard Bauckham, *Jesus and the Eyewitnesses* (Eerdmans, 2006), p. 506.

8. But hasn't the Bible been changed?

1. Dan Brown, *The Da Vinci Code* (Doubleday, 2003), p. 231.

2. Christopher Hitchens, *God Is Not Great* (Atlantic, 2007), p. 110.

3. Bart Ehrman, *Misquoting Jesus: The Story Behind Who Changed the Bible and Why?* (HarperOne, 2007), p. 207.

4. It is worth noting that Erhman himself would say that it was not the issue of the reliability of the Bible that actually led to the loss of his evangelical faith, but the problem of suffering – not an intellectual problem, but a moral one. In my first book, *What Kind of God?*, I deal with this and a number of other moral objections. For an interesting discussion, see http://www.premierchristianradio.com/Shows/Saturday/Unbelievable/

Episodes/Unbelievable-3-Jan-2009-Misquoting-Jesus-Ehrman-
Williams.

5. The three main areas where it appears that extra text may have
been added later to the New Testament are in Mark 16:9–20,
John 7:53 – 8:11 and 1 John 5:7. These have long been
acknowledged, and there has been no cover-up. It is worth
noting that these don't change the teaching of the New
Testament. Even without the longer ending of Mark, the
resurrection is clearly taught. The principles that we see in the
story in John 8 are found elsewhere. The removal of the
reference to the Trinity (God as one being, yet expressed in three
persons) in 1 John 5:7 does not destroy the doctrine. No doctrine
is based on a single verse anyway, and the idea of God as Trinity
is clearly revealed throughout the New Testament. I know of
no Christian today whose reason for believing in the Trinity is
1 John 5:7. More significantly, when Christians first formulated
the doctrine of the Trinity, it had nothing to do with this verse,
but rather their understanding of God's revelation in Jesus.

6. See Keith Small, *Holy Books Have a History* (Avant, 2010), p. 68.

7. Uthman c653 Al-Hajjaj c705; see Keith Small, *Holy Books Have a
History* (Avant, 2010), p. 69.

8. Keith Small, *Holy Books Have a History* (Avant, 2010), p. 59.

9. Ibid, p. 70.

10. Ibid, p. 78.

11. There are several reasons for this. First, The Muratorian
Fragment is the copy of a document from the second century
that lists all four Gospels and most of the other New Testament
books. Secondly, Irenaeus (second century) refers to the four
Gospels in his writings and maintains that they are firmly
established as the four points on the compass. The New
Testament Gospels are widely alluded to and quoted in the
writings of early Christians. In comparison, the other gospels
are not referenced or treated with this kind of authority.

204 | BUT IS IT TRUE?

12. Some may also raise the question of the Apocrypha – a collection of additional books found in Orthodox and Catholic Bibles, but not Protestant ones. However, this is not important to the New Testament, as all the books are from the time before Jesus, and it has no bearing on the main teaching of Christianity. Their main value is on shedding light on the 400-year period between the Old and New Testaments.

9. But aren't there many different opinions about who Jesus was?

1. The reality is that Jesus was probably born in 7 BC. This discrepancy in the dating was due to the sixth-century monk who got his calculations wrong!
2. Matthew 5:41.
3. Matthew 5:39.
4. Mark 1:22.
5. Matthew 5:43–48.
6. Matthew 18:21–22.
7. Matthew 5:21–22.
8. Matthew 5:28.
9. G. K. Chesterton, *What's Wrong with the World* (Serenity, 2009), p. 28.
10. Luke 23:34.
11. Matthew 8:3; Mark 1:41; Luke 5:13.
12. Mark 6:30–44.
13. Luke 8:1–3.
14. Luke 10:38–42.
15. Luke 18:1–8; 21:1–4.
16. John 8:46.
17. Sahih Bukhari, Hadith 5832.
18. Matthew 6:12.
19. Luke 14:1.
20. John 2:1–12.
21. Matthew 11:19.

22. Luke 15:1.

23. Matthew 23:1–39.

24. Matthew 21:12–17.

25. *The Spectator*, 22 April 2006: http://www.spectator.co.uk/columnists/matthew-parris/7667978/beware-i-would-say-to-believers-the-patronage-of-unbelievers/.

26. The following are just a few examples of the prophecies that Jesus fulfilled. He was born in Bethlehem (Micah 5:2), of a virgin (Isaiah 7:14), in the line of Abraham (Genesis 12:3). He would spend time in Egypt (Hosea 11:1), be rejected by his own people (Psalm 69:8), bring light to Galilee (Isaiah 9:1–2), be praised by little children (Psalm 8:2). He would then be betrayed (Psalm 41:9), falsely accused (Psalm 35:11), and would be silent before his accusers (Isaiah 53:7). He would be crucified with criminals (Isaiah 53:12), given vinegar to drink (Psalm 69:21), pierced (Zechariah 12:10) and buried with the rich (Isaiah 53:9).

27. http://sciencespeaks.dstoner.net/Christ_of_Prophecy.html.

28. John 14:6.

29. Matthew 24:35.

30. John 11:25.

31. Matthew 7:1; John 5:22.

32. John 20:24–28.

33. Mark 2:1–12.

34. John 10:38; 14:11.

35. John 9:1–12.

36. Mark 7:31–37.

37. Mark 5:1–20.

38. Matthew 14:13–21.

39. Mark 4:35–41.

40. John 11:38–44; 20:1–31.

41. Mark 4:41.

42. 'Christ' was the Greek translation of the Hebrew word 'Messiah', which means 'anointed one' or 'king'.

43. John 8:58.
44. This reference is from a letter by the Roman Governor Pliny the Younger to the Emperor Trajan, in which he asks for advice on what to do with the Christians in his jurisdiction of Bithynia (present-day Turkey). See Pliny the Younger, *Letters*, 10.96–97.
45. https://en.wikipedia.org/wiki/Alexamenos_graffito#/media/File:AlexGraffito.svg.
46. Mark 8:31–33.
47. Mark 10:45.
48. Mark 7:14–15.
49. The Queen's Christmas Broadcast, 2011: http://www.royal.gov.uk/ImagesandBroadcasts/TheQueensChristmasBroadcasts/ChristmasBroadcasts/TheQueensChristmasBroadcast.aspx.

10. But isn't Jesus dead and gone?

1. 1 Corinthans 15:17.
2. http://www.protorah.com/go-delusion-debate-dawkins-lennox-transcript/.
3. Acts 17:32.
4. In this sense, it is very similar to the argument over fine-tuning that we looked at in chapter 2. Few, if any, cosmologists doubt that the universe is finely tuned to support life. The difference of opinion is over how we interpret the evidence. Does it point us to God?
5. Dominic Crossan, *Jesus: A Revolutionary Biography* (HarperCollins, 1991), p. 145.
6. Matthew 28:11–15.
7. Talmud, Sotah 19a.
8. Josephus, *Antiquities* 4.8.15, tr. and ed. by William Whiston, *The Life and Work of Flavius Josephus* (Hendrikson, 1987 [1737]).
9. Luke 24:11.
10. 1 Corinthians 15:3–8.
11. Lüdemann wrote, 'Paulus . . . betont . . . dass er dies selbst – wohl bald nach seiner Bekehrung (etwa 32 n.Chr.) – empfangen

habe (Vers 3b)': *Die Aufstehung Jesus – Fiktion oder Wirklichkeit? Ein Streitgespräch* (Basel, 2001), p. 73. This work is available only in German, but a translation would read, 'Paul . . . emphasizes . . . that he received this himself (v. 3b) – probably shortly after his conversion (around AD 32) (*The Resurrection of Jesus – Fiction or Reality? A Disputation*).

12. See Gary Habermas and Michael Licona, *The Case for the Resurrection of Jesus* (Kregel, 2004), pp. 56–62.

13. Ibid., p. 59.

14. Rudolf Bultmann, *The New Testament and Mythology* (Harper and Row, 1961), p. 42.

15. Gerd Lüdermann, *What Really Happened to Jesus? A Historical Approach to the Resurrection* (Westminster John Knox, 1995), p. 80.

16. Acts 9:1–19; 22:1–13; 26:1–32.

17. Mark 3:21, 31; 6:3–4; John 7:5.

18. Tacitus, *Annals*, 15:44.

19. Baptism was a symbol of identification with the death and resurrection of Jesus. In sharing bread and wine, they didn't just remember that Jesus had died, but that he was alive and connected to them by his Spirit.

20. Surah 4:157–158. However, Surah 3:54 appears to indicate that Jesus would die.

21. For further discussion of this, see Gary Habermas and Michael Licona, *The Case for the Resurrection of Jesus* (Kregel, 2004), p. 102.

22. Acts 2:32.

23. Matthew 28:11–15.

24. Charles W. Colson, *Loving God* (Marshall, Morgan & Scott, 1984), p. 69.

25. C. F. D. Moule, *The Phenomenon of the New Testament* (SCM, 1967), pp. 3, 13.

26. Tom Wright, Appendix B, in Anthony Flew, *There Is a God* (HarperOne, 2007), p. 210.

Conclusion: So what if it's true?

1. Acts 17:31.
2. Mark 7:14–15.
3. Alexander Solzhenitsyn, *The Gulag Archipelago, 1918–1956, Volume 1* (Westview Press, 1974), p. 168.
4. Richard Dawkins, *The God Delusion* (Bantam, 2006), p. 253.
5. Luke 15:11–32.
6. Bertrand Russell, 'The Free Man's Worship' (1903): http://users.drew.edu/~jlenz/br-fmw.html.
7. Quoted from a talk by Christian apologist, Michael Ramsden.
8. C. S. Lewis, *Reflections on the Psalms* (Brace & Co., 1958), pp. 93–97.
9. *The Lord of the Rings: The Two Towers* (2002), film directed by Peter Jackson.

Afterword: What next?

1. http://www.telegraph.co.uk/news/religion/11381589/Watch-Stephen-Fry-brands-God-utterly-utterly-evil.html.

Lightning Source UK Ltd.
Milton Keynes UK
UKHW020641300721
388036UK00014B/1427